# Dating Fun for Couples

400 creative dating ideas for you to try

Vern A. Jensen, PhD

ISBN: 1495905349
ISBN 13: 9781495905346
Library of Congress Control Number: 2014902887
CreateSpace Independent Publishing Platform
North Charleston, South Carolina

# Dedication

To Migsie,

My wife and sweetheart!

With gratitude for the many years

of dating fun,

that have made our marriage so happy,

creative, and fulfilling.

For all the impromptu dates,

those special romantic getaways,

and everything in between.

You are indeed,

The love of my life!

# Contents

# Introduction

Recently, my wife and I were driving home from a short vacation, and we began discussing some of the things we had done in our dating life. She started writing down some of the fun and romance we've shared together, and we had listed over a hundred different dating experiences before we arrived home. We had made a commitment at the beginning of our marriage to have at least one date every week. While some of them were more memorable than others, we can say we have had a date nearly every week of our more than thirty-year marriage. No wonder we have such a great relationship!

For many years now, I have counseled and talked to thousands of couples, most of whom have had less than happy marriages. When I have asked about their "date life" they often draw a complete blank, or say something like, "I don't think we have had a date so far this year," or "We haven't had a date in months." Is it any wonder that these marriages are in serious trouble. It is interesting to me how much creativity and determination goes into the dating experience before couples get married and how little goes into it after marriage. It gets even worse as children come and couples get preoccupied with family issues, business, and just plain busyness that is not in the category of dating. When I talk with friends of ours who have reasonably good marriages but are drifting apart or becoming more conflicted in their relationships, I urge them to start dating at least once a week. Almost invariably they have reported later that their relationship was now much better, and they were enjoying each other again.

Another issue is the lack of creativity in their dating. In talking with couples, I have found that one of the problems is that they don't have much fun on their dates. They'll maybe do dinner and a movie once every month or two, but really don't have any great ideas for dates that could be more fun, more romantic, or more fulfilling. Some complain that they don't have enough money and it just "costs too much to date." Others say that they only do things together as a family or just the things their kids want to do—no real couple time.

In view of these issues, I have decided to offer this short book of dating ideas to help inspire creative ideas in various categories: free dates, cheap dates, romantic dates, fun dates, indoor dates, outdoor dates, educational dates, group dates, faith-building dates, and special getaways fill the following pages. While the ideas offered here suggest activities that you can do together, the most important thing is not the activity in itself but what you share with each other on the date. If you use your date to talk about family problems or argue and fuss about things, you might as well have stayed home and not wasted the time. If you fill at least some of the time sharing more deeply, remembering special times together, laughing, being silly, and just plain having fun together, your dating will be something to look forward to and less like a trip to the dentist.

In other words, you might choose an activity from the list of suggestions, but choose to share in a totally different way while on your date. Mix and match the ideas as much as you wish. The most important thing is to make a commitment to have a date every week and let no excuse get in the way.

Early in our marriage, while we were struggling to make a living in our business, I received a call from a TV station manager who wanted me to come on TV and talk about our business. I was excited and asked when. They wanted me the next Friday night. I asked if it could be another time but was told it had to be that night. I thought for a moment, realizing how much that could mean to our business, and then replied, "No, I have another commitment." My wife overheard the conversation and wondered what in the world was more important than this business opportunity. After I hung up, I explained, "It was our date night." If we had allowed something else to be more important than our commitment once, then we would have set the precedent to allow it to happen again. If you don't make dating a commitment, then it won't happen because there is always something that can interfere. After that, your marriage will be less fun, less romantic, and less fulfilling day-by-day, as you hardly notice what is happening.

Some of you reading this book may still be single. That's great! Use the ideas in this book while you are still dating, but remember to continue dating once you get in a permanent relationship. It will be even more important then.

I believe when God created the experience we call marriage, He had in mind that we would have happy and fulfilling marriages, that we would be connected by spending time together, enjoying each other, and having fun together. He never intended that it become dull or boring and certainly not conflicted. We are to become friends, partners, and lovers. Remember, your relationship, married or single, can be as great as you want it to be or as dull and boring as you let it become. It is your choice!

Enjoy the journey ahead!

Vern A. Jensen, PhD

**Instructions**: This is not a book to be read. It is a resource manual to be used to stimulate your creativity in dating. One of the best ways to use this would be to skim through the different sections with your partner, and select several ideas from each section and make a note of them. Share this with your partner, and begin to identify eight to ten ideas that you both like. Then get out your calendar and begin scheduling those dates. When your list is running out, repeat the process. Some of these ideas have been listed in more than one section. Many could have been. Some of these ideas will seem ridiculous to you or too silly to consider, but they might get you thinking in some new directions. Don't always try to do the grown-up thing. In case you haven't noticed, kids have a lot more fun than grown-ups. That is really sad. Do some things just for pure fun, others for more significant meaning, and others to stimulate your faith and your desire to serve. As you do more and more different things, new things, you will enrich your relationship in many meaningful ways. Just enjoy the journey!

# Free or Cheap Dates

One of the important matters couples bring up when I challenge them to have a date every week is the cost. Most dates cost money, and many couples, especially in their early years, don't have a lot of extra money. Even if the date is free, when you have to pay a baby-sitter it is still expensive. Let me say two things. First, most couples have some friends that would be happy to baby-sit for each other, trading nights. Or, develop a co-op where several couples agree to sit for each other, so each couple can have a date. Second, on a more dismal note, think about the cost of a separation and divorce. I have seen it happen so many times as couples gradually drift away and lose the joy and romance of the relationship. Put money into your budget for baby-sitting, and treat it with the same respect as a college fund or retirement account. If you can't find another couple to trade with, then still make it a priority to have a weekly date. It can make all the difference in your marriage.

**Amusement Park** Go to a local amusement park, carnival, or county fair. Local church festivals or carnivals are a great option. They are free to get in, so you can spend your money on games or food.

**Arcade** Go to a local arcade. This doesn't have to be expensive, but go without kids and just be kids for the date. Challenge each other to see who is the greatest as you try to impress each other with your score, or just laugh at each other in an

1

attempt to win it all. Let the loser buy the winner a hot dog or something to drink.

**Aquarium** Check out all the animals and species that live in water. If this is too costly, volunteer at your local animal shelter and play with the pets.

**Band Concert** Find a local school that has a band concert and go to enjoy or just to support the school band.

**Be a City Nomad** Buy a day pass for the bus and take the public transit around your city with your spouse. You'll see sights and sounds that you wouldn't ordinarily notice while speeding through in your car. Jump off whenever you see something that catches your fancy. You never know what you'll discover or rediscover! Share with each other what you are experiencing in this venture.

**Be a Tourist** Pretend you are a tourist in your own town (or a nearby town) and see the sites and do the things that a tourist might do. You may discover some neat things you have overlooked, or it might give you an opportunity to share experiences you have had before. The list of possibilities is nearly endless. Get a brochure from the Chamber of Commerce, if necessary, for some ideas.

**Blindfold Date** Blindfold your date for a surprise dinner, and take them to McDonald's or another fast-food restaurant. Plan ahead and make your table really fancy with a tablecloth, nice dishes and cups, and perhaps some candlelight. Craft your own fancy menu, and enlist some friends to help and be your servers.

**Bonfire Fun** Build a bonfire complete with marshmallows ready for toasting. If that is not so easy, then try building a smaller fire in a fire pit, and see who toasts the best marsh-mallow without burning it.

**Bookstore Fun** Go to your favorite bookstore, especially one that has a café as a part of it. Grab a coffee or latte and find a special section to browse. You might go to the travel section and plan an imaginary trip that perhaps later can become real. Or you could go to the children's section and read a couple of your favorite stories to each other. If the bookstore has a music section, browse through some of your favorite musicians, and maybe pick out a romantic album you can take home for another date. This idea could be used for several different dates.

**Brew a Beverage** Try your hand at making cappuccinos, fla-vored ice tea, or brew your own beer. Get out the blender and try a new smoothie. You may find a new favorite.

**Build Something** Think together about something you can build. It could be a food, like a pizza or an ice cream sundae, or something structural with blocks, boxes, or nontraditional building materials. Let your creativity be at work, and laugh at some of the possibilities. You may well learn something new about your partner.

**Car Wash** Wash your cars together and have a little fun with the water hose. Get some fresh towels, and help dry each other off. It's always fun to play with water. Then, in your newly cleaned car, go out and get something to eat. Maybe try a drive-in; you may not be at your most presentable but your car will be.

**Childhood Games** Play a game from your childhood—croquet, badminton, hide-and-seek, or miniature golf. Reminisce and be playful together.

**Coffee Stroll** Grab a cup of coffee or some other drink and take a leisurely stroll through your neighborhood. See how many of the neighbors you know or if there's someone new you would like to meet. Just share this time with your loved one. Or go to a local park and do the same thing.

**College Sports** Grab tickets to a local college sports game, and go cheer for the home team. Even a high school game will work. You might even become fans and get season tickets for the next year.

**Comedy Club** Grab a few laughs at a local comedy club or go find a funny movie. Spend some time just laughing together over something silly.

**Costume Fun** Pretend you are children again as each of you create a costume using items you find in your house. The costume can be funny, scary, or even depict a certain character. Then get together to reveal what you have created, and tell your story as you share a meal.

**Coupon Date** Have a coupon date. Go through the local newspaper or magazine together and find coupons to use on your cheap date. Restaurants and convenience stores often have a stack of local magazines with coupons.

**Farmer's Market** Visit your local farmer's market, and get some fresh produce that you can use to make a special vegetable dinner. Then go home and share in preparing it. Add whatever else you want to make it a special dinner.

**Favorites Night** You and your partner each plan a date around the other's favorite things. Do your best to include as many clothes, games, sports, foods, or activities that your partner likes. On the next date, reverse the plan and have your partner do the same for you. Alternatively, you could just plan one date that combines a few of your favorite things. For example, perhaps integrate one of your favorite activities with one of your partner's favorite places to eat. The possibilities are endless!

**Guess What?** Go to a fast-food restaurant and order a random variety of items. Then put blindfolds on each other, and guess what the food you randomly ordered is. It's super fun, and you get to eat at the same time!

**Have a Board Night** Pick your favorite board game and spend the evening playing together. Share childhood memories of games you used to play and who used to win all the time. Monopoly, Candy Land, and Sorry are a few ideas, just for starters.

**Karaoke** Find a bar with karaoke, and take turns impressing each other. You might even go for a duet, and have fun laughing at yourselves. Otherwise, just have fun watching others try to impress.

**Leaf Raking** Rake leaves together. Make a big pile and jump in them. Let go of any inhibitions about being neat and tidy. Don't have any fallen leaves? Find someone who does and volunteer to rake their yard.

**Musicals/Plays** If you want to do this for less, choose a high school play or musical. If you have a local community theater, see if they will sell tickets to a dress rehearsal. If you have some extra money to spend you can always hit the high-price theaters.

**New Restaurant** Make reservations for dinner at a restaurant you've always wanted to go to, and decide on something special to wear as you celebrate just being together.

**Outdoor Concert** Find an outdoor concert with cheap tickets. Grab your lawn chairs for a fun summer date night.

**Paintball** Play paintball! This is nearly free if you have your own equipment; if not, opt for a water-gun fight instead. See who has the best aim. Designate one of you as the villain and go after each other.

**Patio Date** Plan an evening "out" as you barbecue your favorite meal, have special beverages, and just enjoy the evening. Maybe extend the date with a fire pit and some shared dreams as you roast marshmallows together.

**People Watching** Go to a public place such as a mall, hotel lobby, or restaurant, and make up stories about the people you see. Create mysterious or humorous story lines about everyone that passes by. Pretend you are a reporter on an important story or a detective on a case. If you see someone who looks troubled, pray for that person, or go and talk to the person and act out your concern.

**Personal Beach Party** Spend the afternoon at the beach with beach chairs, blankets, and a picnic basket with all the trimmings. Don't forget the sunscreen!

**Pet Store** Visit a pet store and check out your favorite animals. Compare notes about any pets you had as children and how you felt about them. Make an agreement before you go that you are only doing this for fun and not buying a pet, no matter how cute, unless this was not the original agreement.

**Photo Albums** Get out the old photo albums and have fun looking at your wedding pictures, childhood photos, or some favorite vacation pictures. Share some stories and memories. If you have your pictures on computers, see if you can project them on your TV, or just snuggle together and watch them on the computer screen.

**Picture Story** Describe your life in pictures by cutting things out of magazines and making a collage. Tell the story you have created.

**Plan Your Next Vacation** Spend the evening talking about where you would like to go. Check out some possibilities on the Internet in order to help you decide. Then, once you decide, find attractions and things to do while you're there.

**Play Bingo** It's surprisingly fun, affordable, and you may even win a little extra money for your next date.

**Playground Fun** Go to a local park and play on the playground. Push each other in the swings or on the merry-go-round. Try bouncing each other off the teeter-totter. Climb on the ropes. Dig in the sand. Pretend you are kids again, and let your inner child come out to play.

**Quarters** Get a roll of quarters, head for the local arcade, and see how much fun you can have playing games together. Or think of how many things you can do with quarters in other places and have a fun time spending your fortune. Have a contest to see who can get the best or most creative item from the twenty-five cent machines (maybe in a shopping mall).

**Restaurant Tour** Go on a restaurant tour on the cheap. Stop in for an appetizer at a few different locations to try out some new foods. Make sure to save room for new desserts as well.

**Ride All Night** Take your date to a theme park on a night where you can purchase unlimited-ride wristbands that will have you sharing rides all night long. Find a quiet place to enjoy the funnel cake or elephant ears. Get a favorite drink with two straws.

**Scary Movie Night** Have a scary movie marathon or just a movie marathon. You could pick a certain actor or actress and watch a couple of movies they star in, either old or new. You could even take turns choosing the movies and have several theme dates.

**Skinny-Dipping** If it's warm outside, go skinny-dipping at your local lake or pool. If it's late enough, other people won't be around.

**Snow Fun** If you live where there is snow, go out and make a snowman together or each of you make one of your own. You might just happen to have a snowball fight along the way and stop to make a few snow angels as you make up. Finish off the date with some hot chocolate or a snack of your choice.

**Stargazing** Locate a dark place on a starry night, bring a blanket, and lie down and watch the stars. Try naming the constellations or give them your own names. Choose a star for each other and give it a special romantic name. Just enjoy a time to relax and be together.

**Story Time** Create a story together by taking turns. Elect one of you to start the story, and leave off in the middle by saying "and then." The other takes up the story until stopping in the middle with another "and then." Keep taking turns. Have some fun laughing at each other's creativity. This continues until someone decides to say "the end." You might try recording your story so you can play it back and continue having fun with it.

**Tech Free** Agree to turn off all technology for the date including cell phones, computers, the TV, and even the lights. Use your imagination to see what's left to do without electricity. Light some candles. See what it's like for a whole evening not to be interrupted by phone calls or emails, and just focus on each other.

**The Ungame** Get a copy of the Ungame and take turns pulling out questions for your partner to answer. (This is simply a collection of cards with different questions that you take turns answering.) Some are silly, some easy, and some quite revealing. See what you can learn about your partner as you share in this way. There are other games with questions that could be used as well, or make up some of your own.

**Time Capsule** Make a time capsule to put in a park (or just in your own backyard) full of pictures and objects that represent your relationship. Then plan to dig it up for a special anniversary.

**Thrift Store Date** Go to a thrift store and set a low budget of five dollars. Pick out something (or things) you can purchase for your partner. It could be something crazy or something sweet. Search the stalls for the perfect five-dollar gift for each other. Unusual or quirky items make good gifts, as do market foods, used CDs, jewelry, books, records, and small antique items. You could pick something to be worn and make your partner wear it home. If the owner's price for that perfect item is more than five dollars, tell him your limit and see if you can talk him down. Lots of ideas here.

**TV Marathon** Get hooked on a new TV series and have a marathon. If the programs are not already running all day, most cable companies have a recorded series of the program that you can watch until you've had enough.

**<u>Waiter's Night</u>** Pick a night to wait on your spouse. You do all the serving as you provide drinks, snacks, and favorite items. Maybe dress for the part with a towel on your arm and a gleam in your eye as you have fun seeing all the things you can do to serve on this date. Then reverse roles on a subsequent date as you have your spouse serve you.

**<u>The Zoo</u>** Visit your local zoo or one in a nearby city. Choose a nice day, and have fun viewing the animals. You will find some interesting animals in their cages—some fierce and others lovable. Feeding the giraffes from a balcony can be a new experience. Pick out your favorite animals and share stories of why you like this animal, or pick the ones you hate and share why. Which one would you least like to meet on a dark night? Which one would you like to take home with you if you could? Which one is your partner most like, and which one are you most like? Careful here, you might have to kiss and make up.

# Focus on the Family Dates

As I was researching some dating ideas, I came across a website from Focus on the Family in Canada. They had some great ideas that they have given me permission to reprint. I'm sure you will find some interesting ones in this list. (Reprinted with permission from fotf.ca, copyright 2013 by Focus on the Family Canada. Several slight changes were made in spelling to make them American English.)

**Adopt an Accent** French is the language of love, but you and your spouse can determine your own accents of amore! Commit to speaking in an accent for your entire date, and go to a restaurant or shopping mall where you know you'll be heard by passersby! Whether your dialect of choice is romantic, quirky, or completely made up, feigning an accent is playful and exciting!

**At-Home Spa** Give your love some tender care by planning a relaxing massage date. To create your at-home spa, set up a quiet room with candles, flowers, light, and classical music. Fill the room with a light scent, preferably an essential oil burning in an infuser. Then, have your spouse lie on the bed with fresh sheets, and begin with a head and neck rub, followed by a back massage. Be sure to take your time and ask your spouse what pressure they prefer and what spots need the most attention. If you want help with your massage skills, there are plenty of books available to give you tips. But don't worry! Whether you know how to give a perfect massage, giving a gift of loving touch is a surefire way to convey love and care to your mate.

**Back to the Dating Days** Think back to some of the earliest dates you went on with your spouse. Set aside an afternoon, evening, or an entire day to recreate these memories. Want to go an extra mile? Bring along a camera and then compare the pictures to the ones you took on those first dates, and celebrate how far you've come in your relationship.

**Backyard Restaurant** A tight budget doesn't mean you can't still go out for dinner. Lay an old sheet down on your backyard or deck, place a couple couch cushions on top of it, and then top it off with a comforter. Make dinner ahead of time and go enjoy a meal on your cushy makeshift restaurant booth. You can even light candles to create a romantic atmosphere.

**Berry Picking** Take your spouse on a berry-picking date and delight in God's artistry and provision. In the summer, many types of berries can be found growing wild in almost every city and local park. Most summer berries thrive well in exposed, sunny places like fields. You're almost certain to find them living happily along riverbanks and abandoned train tracks. For your date, bring plastic containers and long-sleeved clothing you don't mind getting stained and ripped. Gloves are also a good idea to protect you from raspberry and blackberry thorns. While you're enjoying all this wonderful fruit, try to find the juiciest, sweetest berries, and give them to your loved one to enjoy. Or, have a contest to see who can pick the most berries or find the biggest one. Then, take your fruit home and eat them fresh with ice cream or on their own. Remember, while it may be tempting to pick all you can of this free fruit, don't go overboard; leave some for others—including the wildlife—to enjoy.

**Blast to the Past** Who knew that looking at old junk could be so fun? Spend the day with your date at a flea market or antique store, and see what kinds of unique and funny items you can find. It's a great way to learn something new about your spouse: you'll never know what stories they may have about an old antique or toy from their parents' childhood.

**Christmas in...August?** Why wait until December to bless your spouse with a special gift? Catch him by surprise with an early Christmas gift! You don't need to spend a lot of money to treat your sweetheart to an unexpected surprise—even something small is bound to impress! Or, plan a day together when you can both exchange gifts, celebrate each other, and thank the Savior for His ever-constant love!

**Comic Couples** When was the last time you and your spouse shared a good laugh? Plan a comedy-themed date with the goal to laugh all evening. Before your date, ask your love to collect silly jokes and think of funny childhood memories to share at dinner. For more laughs during your meal, play the straight-faced game—see who can hold their serious expression without laughing first. Try it multiple times: winner gets a big bite off the other's plate! If you don't care about the other diners watching your silliness, sit side-by-side so you can take photos of yourselves making the goofiest faces. Top off the evening with a side-splitting time at a local improv show.

**Creative Chatter Around the Christmas Tree** As you're setting up your Christmas tree this year, share some of your favorite family traditions with each other. Can't think of a tradition? Tell your spouse about your most memorable Christmas as a child.

**Dates that Support Your Resolution(s)** Are two of your resolutions to go on more adventures and save money? Plan a date night using online coupon sites like Groupon, Dealfind or LivingSocial. Look for discounts to local restaurants, art studios, dance classes, or live entertainment. You'll save money, create memories, and discover more about the area where you and your spouse live.

**Dinner Date via Garage Sale** Gather up some stuff that you've had for ages but rarely use—kitchen supplies, chairs, lamps, books, and movies. Have a Saturday garage sale and use whatever money you make to go out for dinner that night—even if just for a fast-food dining experience.

**Drive-in Movie Night in Your Car** Pick a movie, charge your laptop or portable DVD player, pack some blankets and snacks, and drive to a favorite park. Enjoy a movie night in the comfort of your own car.

**Duet? Do It!** Maybe you won't win this season's TV talent show, but you and your spouse can be superstars in your living room! Choose a favorite song and look up the lyrics online. Spend an evening at home learning to sing the song with your spouse. Sing with gusto, laughing as you squeak on the high notes. If you're great singers, try squeaking anyway—aim for playfulness, not perfection! For a bigger challenge, attempt a two-part harmony.

**Encouragement via Driftwood** Find a flat piece of scrap wood and use a permanent marker to write out your favorite Bible verses. Take it to a nearby beach, river, or lake and toss it in the water. This may be of great encouragement to whoever finds it later on.

**Festive Photography** During the Christmas season, the streets are usually decked with lovely decorations. What better time than now to try a creative photography date with your spouse?

Armed with a digital camera and bundled in warm clothes, set off together to one of your favorite spots in town. But instead of shooting photos of each other in standard poses, find items you think describe the other person or select an abstract theme (like "irreplaceable" or "hope"). For example, if you choose to describe your wife, you might take a picture of a glittering ornament, one of her favorite things, or even a collection of your wife's facial expressions—just for fun. Be creative and think outside the box! Afterward, find a cozy café, and get to know your mate's creative side as you share your images over a steamy cup of hot chocolate.

**Follow the Stars** On a clear, summer night, take your love on a stargazing adventure. Start by picking a big, bright star, and follow it on foot while holding hands and talking. At any point, stop for ice cream or dessert, at a park, or anything you come across along the way. Follow your star until you can't follow it anymore, then pick another star to follow. For a surprise, take your spouse to a different neighborhood or part of town, and use this activity to explore it together!

**Four Festive Fall Ideas** As the air takes on a crisp nip, celebrate God's handiwork in the changing seasons with four fun ideas perfect for the start of fall.

**Corncob Feeder** Make a corncob bird feeder, then spend an afternoon together as birds flock to your backyard. The birds will appreciate the gesture as natural food sources dwindle. To make a feeder, eat all the corn off of the cob and let it dry for a day or two. Spread peanut butter on the cob, then stick birdseed into the peanut butter. Hang it from a tall tree branch or the eaves of your roof.

**Corn Maze** Explore a corn maze. The sense of adventure can be a great bonding experience. If you have older children, the twisting corridors of the maze can also be entertaining for them while giving mom and dad some alone time.

**Pumpkin Farm** Head to a pumpkin farm and pick out a couple of pumpkins to carve together. It's budget-friendly and lets you show off your creative side. For example, each of you could carve a scene from one of your first dates, or inscribe a scripture that reflects a quality you see in your spouse. Remember to save the seeds, which make for an easy snack. Scatter the seeds in a single layer onto a baking sheet and roast them in an oven set to 165°F for 15 minutes.

**Scarecrow** Build a friendly scarecrow with each other. It can lend a festive, fun look to your front yard or patio. Stuff old clothes with hay or straw, available for free or at a low cost at many farms, feed stores, and hobby outlets. Tie the ends of the garments shut with twine. For a head, use a small pumpkin or a pillowcase.

**Go Geocaching** Geocaching uses your handheld GPS device or smartphone and turns the world into one giant treasure hunt. This adventurous date idea gives you a chance to enjoy the spring weather. Visit geocaching.com to get started.

**Go Off Broadway…Even Further** Forget expensive Broadway tickets, or even Off Broadway shows. Instead, support off-Off Broadway: your local community theater. You'll find the classic shows you both love, plus modern plays, and all at a wallet-friendly price.

**Harvest Bounty** Being harvest season, fall offers plenty of options for a great date with your spouse. Crisp, cool weather is the perfect temperature for a bike ride through leaf-covered paths or a stroll through a wooded area bursting with bright red, yellow, and orange trees. Or, take a drive out of town for a mini-getaway to explore the countryside while keeping the destination a secret from your spouse. Places to visit could be an apple orchard or festival where you can sample local varieties and fresh apple cider. Another idea is to drop by a fall fair, which usually showcases local livestock, produce, baking, and crafts. Better yet, sample the cooking contest entries and taste some of the best apple pie, home-made preserves, pies, and breads in the county. Afterward, hop on a hayride with your spouse to enjoy life and each other at a slower pace. Whatever you choose to do for your fall date, you'll find plenty to see, taste, and do during this season of harvest abundance.

**Hello Again** Remember the early days when you and your spouse were first dating? Recreate the excitement of your first encounter with a date pretending you don't know each other. For example, set a time and place with your date for your "chance" encounter. On the big night, dress to impress before you head out. When at your meeting location, keep an eye out for your love and be ready with some smooth (or corny) pick-up lines. Then, spend the evening flirting and getting to know each other all over again!

**Hop on, Hop off the Bus** When the weather outside is frightful and going out by car provides a challenge, try a low-key date using the public transit in your city or town. Rapid transit, buses, or tram cars are an excellent alternative to driving and allow for more focused conversation without the distractions of traffic. When it's not rush hour, you'll be more likely to find a double seat to yourselves. Hop on a route you've never taken before or explore an area of town you don't visit often. And since no one is driving (or backseat driving), you can both kick back and enjoy the sights as someone else takes care of dodging traffic. If there's a street you know with lots of places to eat and things to see, add spontaneity to your date by getting off any time there's a place either of you want to visit. Then, take the time to explore the area before hopping back on the bus and discovering your next venue.

**Literary Adventures** For a simple date, cozy up with your spouse at your local library. But instead of going your separate ways to find a book for yourselves; both of you will choose ones you think the other would enjoy. Mix it up! Choose your favorite books, ones you enjoyed as a child (like picture books and young readers), or even books you've never read before. Reading something new helps spark new ideas, new thoughts and reactions. You never know: your husband may end up loving your favorite, *Pride and Prejudice* (albeit, secretly), and your wife may come to share your childhood love for *The Hobbit*. Whether you end up loving or disliking a book, both of you will have engaged in sharing yourselves with each other. It may be a great way to sharpen your minds, but it also provides a chance for you to flex those communication and imagination muscles.

**Lunch Date** Fall can often be dreary as the rain moves in. Break up the midday gloom with a lunch date with your spouse. If you're fortunate enough to live close by your spouse's workplace, take them out to a cozy café or restaurant. But instead of treating it merely as lunch, treat your outing as a date—meaning, get dressed up a little, flirt with each other, and avoid talking about what needs to get done at home. Why wait until evening to reconnect with your love, when you can do it at noon?

**Make a 2015 Time Capsule** Fill a glass jar with objects that represent your year with your spouse. Items can include ticket stubs from a favorite movie, restaurant receipts from memorable dates, or photos from a vacation. Bury it in your yard and then dig it up the following year. This is a fun way to relive your shared memories each year!

**The More the Merrier** A double date with a twist! Have the husbands become one date-planning team and the wives become another. With your date-planning partner, combine your ideas for a super-secret creative date for your spouses. Who knows what new and exciting ideas you'll come up when you brainstorm date ideas with a friend? Throw in a little friendly competition by setting the expectation that each team should try to outdo the other on their turns to impress! This way, your double dates might just get better and better each time!

**A Movie under the Stars** In today's multi-screen movie theaters, it's next to impossible to avoid the gaggles of teens and crowds of parents with young kids. Instead of facing the bustle of an evening film showing, try a drive-in theater where you and your spouse can experience the big screen from the privacy of your own car. Even if you don't have bench seats, you can still cuddle up in your vehicle under cozy blankets. If you own a station wagon or SUV, take advantage of your trunk space by turning it into your own romantic theater seating. Back your car into your spot, pop open the trunk (while turning off all inside lights), and lay down blankets and pillows. The same can be done with a hatch-less truck. Or, bring lawn chairs to prop by your car and have a true outdoor movie-watching experience. Either way, watching a movie under the stars can refresh your indoor theater routine and give you ample excuse to stay up late and snuggle.

**Pick a New Restaurant** Do an Internet search of restaurants in or near your neighborhood. Try some place neither of you have eaten at before. This is a fun way to explore different cuisines—you may even find a new favorite!

**Picks of the Season** Fall is here—and so are the apples and pumpkins! During the crisp, autumn months, take your spouse on an apple or pumpkin-picking date. Experience together the many sights, smells, and flavors of the various varieties, as many places offer tasting samples. You'll both learn a thing or two about fall produce and you might come home with plenty of cider, pies, and other tasty goodies to enjoy with your love.

**Plant a Garden** Doing a creative task together helps couples grow closer. Create a backyard garden or, if you live in an apartment, a container garden. Enjoy the creative process of shopping for seeds or plants and working the soil.

**Playground Date** Remember how fun it was to go down a slide as a kid or see how high you could swing? Fill two travel mugs with your favorite warm beverage, find a nearby park with a playground, and let loose your inner child! Share your childhood playground memories with each other. You may learn something new about your spouse!

**Quick Road Trip** Road trips don't always have to be extravagant. Drive to a nearby neighborhood. When you get to an intersection, one of you will say "straight," "left," or "right." At the next intersection, the other person will decide. Continue for as long as you like. Enjoy this time exploring your surroundings and creating memories as a couple. (You may need a GPS to find your way home, or just have fun being lost.)

**Real Estate Date** Whether you're on the house hunt, or comfortably settled in your home, perusing real estate listings with your spouse is free, fun, and a great way to spark conversation! From home or a coffee shop, search online real estate websites such as Realtor.com. Browse a variety of price ranges and property sizes, and brainstorm your plans and preferences for the architecture, interior design, and landscaping of your dream home!

**Row, Row, Row a Boat** One of the great things about summer is that the evenings stay bright. Take your spouse for an evening paddle in a canoe, paddleboat, or double kayak. Many lakeside and seaside marinas rent boats by the hour and provide all you need, from life jackets to paddles, for your water adventure. Pack a snack and choose a destination where you can enjoy your time together at a park or on an island or isolated beach. If it's warm enough, go for a swim or just enjoy the solitude of your location together.

**Sensory Surprises** Surprise your spouse with a different kind of picnic. Gather your loved one's favorite foods, and even some unusual or uncommon foods—ones that your spouse may never have tried (but which you think he'll enjoy). Find a quiet place, such as a park, the beach, or even your backyard, and blindfold your spouse. Make sure he can't peek! Then, feed him a piece of food and have him describe what kinds of flavors, textures, and memories he experiences. Don't let him guess what the food is until he's shared his observations. Your spouse's different reactions, comments, and guesses provide opportunities for great dialogue and conversation (especially if your spouse thinks an olive tastes like fish and reminds him of an eyeball). With the new foods, you get to know your spouse better, and while feeding him his favorites, you'll remind him that he's worth being known and loved. To spice things up, take turns eating and feeding.

**Shall We Dance?** Great for double dates or just the two of you, dancing lessons can be a lot of fun and inexpensive. By nature, dancing is a romantic activity where you can spend plenty of time in close proximity with your spouse while establishing a connection in your movements. Formal dancing lessons can cost more, but many community centers offer informal drop-in lessons for beginners wanting to learn more traditional folk dances, such as Scottish Ceilidh (pronounced "kay-lee") dancing, square, or line dancing. Some locations even offer drop-in beginner lessons for slightly more complicated dances like swing and salsa dancing. Even if you feel insecure about your coordination, taking your loved one dancing is a creative way to interact with your spouse, hone your verbal and nonverbal communication skills, and have fun. Like marriage, dancing requires both of you to learn your individual roles, which you must then learn to use together in performing the dance. Most importantly, success in dancing relies on attentively listening to your partner's physical cues and verbal instructions. These are definitely useful skills to practice and apply to marriage! Remember, it's not about how coordinated you are, but how much fun you have in the process together.

**Silly Snow Scenes** After a fresh snowfall of packing snow, try a creative date with your love by making snow scenes in a field or park. Pack a thermos full of hot chocolate, get bundled up, and head outside for some silly fun! Instead of building the traditional snowman, create a scene that tells a funny story or choose a scene from a favorite book or play. Whether or not you possess artistic skills, you'll get to admire your collaborative handiwork with a cup of hot cocoa in the end.

**Spice It Up!** If you're bored of your recipe repertoire at home, take this opportunity to learn how to make new and exciting dishes with your spouse. Try community center cooking classes that offer different ethnic foods and spend each week learning something new to try at home with your spouse. Learning a new skill, plus having the added bonus of tasting the outcome of your efforts, can spice up your weekly routine—and your relationship!

**<u>Springtime Blooms</u>** With the snow melting and flowers now appearing, take your loved one on a date to your local botanical gardens, parks, or plant nurseries. Trade the dreariness of winter for the colorful offerings of spring's first blooms. If visiting a botanical garden, find out what is growing there beforehand and ask your date to learn the names of the flowers. Then, during your date, see who can identify the most plants. Or if you plan to visit a nursery, take a few seedlings home with you and plant them together in your garden to enjoy.

**<u>Summertime Festivals</u>** With great summer weather comes outdoor festivals, providing creative options for a date with your spouse. Many towns and cities often hold different cultural events during the summer, like jazz and folk festivals, fireworks shows, ethnic celebrations, free outdoor concerts, or movies under the stars. Some cities even hold summer night markets where street vendors sell food and interesting knick-knacks for a bargain. Of course, events will vary according to where you live. Start by doing an Internet search for what's happening in your area, then make plans with your spouse to experience some new festivities together. Bring a blanket or your walking shoes, and enjoy what your town has to offer under the long summer sun.

**<u>Surprise Date Adventures</u>** Keep your spouse guessing by turning date night into a surprise adventure. To begin, make a set of cards (either decorated and written by hand or done on the computer) with one activity listed on each. For example, one could list a movie, and the others could list a restaurant, a dessert café, or a stop by his or her favorite store to pick out a small treat. Each card would then be sealed in an envelope. Present the envelopes to your date and have them choose one out of your hand. Whatever they pick, do it! Repeat the process until all the date options have been chosen.

**Thrift Store Makeover** Go to a local thrift store and pick out a piece of furniture (bookcase, end table, picture frame, etc.). Next, buy a can of spray paint to match your find to your house's style. Sand down the surface of your purchase, paint it, and let it dry. You'll then have a new piece of decor that looks good as new—and it costs next to nothing!

**Travel Vicariously through Film** Do you and your spouse have a favorite travel destination? Still planning a dream vacation? Find a movie set in the country or city of your choice, make some classic movie snacks, and travel vicariously through the film.

**A Trip down Memory Lane** Help your spouse get to know you even better by sharing with her some of your favorite spots from the past and the memories that you associate with them. If you live in the same town where you grew up, bring her to your favorite childhood haunts—whether a pond, playground, or corner store. Other ideas include: your favorite high school hangouts, a walk through your college or university campus, the special place you used to go to spend quiet time with God, and so on.

**A Valentine's Surprise** Are you looking for a creative Valentine's date idea beyond just a dinner and a movie? Add some excitement to your special night by planning a surprise scavenger hunt for your love. Before leaving for work in the morning, give him or her the first clue, and tell them not to open it until they get home or until a certain time. Then, plant their favorite treats, special gifts, and love notes around the house stashed with the next clues, which will eventually indicate the restaurant where you'll be waiting with flowers.

**Watch a Moonrise** September is the last month of summer. Take advantage of the warm evenings before we enter the crisp days of fall. Pack up a blanket, some hot chocolate, and snacks and take your spouse to a nearby park or open hill to watch a moonrise. Check when this month's moon will be full and plan accordingly.

**<u>Wireless Date Night</u>** Go out on a dinner date and turn your phones to silent. Don't check your phones until you leave the restaurant. Enjoy a distraction-free date and get to know your spouse even better.

# Creative, Fun Dates

Some dates are more creative than others. They involve making an effort to put your own creativity into the date. This may help you to learn and appreciate some gifting in your partner that you may not have known before. All dates have some creativity involved unless you do exactly the same thing over and over again. When you do new things, what you share is always new and creative—new ideas, new feelings, new talents, and new experiences. Be creative, playful, simple, or romantic. It doesn't matter as long as you're talking, laughing, and celebrating life together.

**Ask Directions** Go around town, perhaps dressed like tourists. Try a funny accent, and start asking people for directions to a place that doesn't exist. "Can you help me find the tower? I am told it is around here somewhere." Or just make up a fictitious destination and ask someone to help you find it.

**Be a Kid Again** Go to a playground and swing, hop on the merry-go-round, fly a kite, feed the ducks, and go out for an ice cream cone.

**Blindfold Miniature Golf** Miniature golf is a fun date in itself, but to switch it up, try putting blindfolded. Blindfold your partner, and then try to guide them to the hole. See who is best at giving directions and who is best at taking them. Enjoy the frustration, and have fun. You may even get a hole in one.

**Boat Show** Find a boat show in your area or go someplace to visit one. Have fun touring the yachts, and imagine what it would be like to live on one. Pretend you are starting out on a cruise around the world, going from one port to the next, and share the journey with your partner. Maybe, one day, you will get a boat and make your dream come true.

**Bucket List** Make a marriage bucket list; a list of things you want to do before you kick the bucket. Think of some important things you want to do in your marriage—special places to visit or specific goals—and make a plan to cross one of the items off your list in the immediate future.

**Camera Time** Grab your cameras or phones, and head out the door. Go somewhere with visual appeal. Start taking pictures of people, sights, scenery, or unusual objects. Go different places. Maybe there will even be a special sunset. Go home and have a picture show. Print several of your favorites, and decide together which picture wins the photo contest.

**Candlelight Dinner** Plan and cook a special meal together. Set the table with your finest of everything, and eat by candlelight. Don't forget the soft music. The dessert can be something special, but don't be in a hurry to get to the dessert. Enjoy the moment!

**Cartoon Date** Get out of bed early on a Saturday morning, still in your pajamas, and choose a cartoon channel that you can watch while you eat your favorite kid's cereal. Take turns picking the channel and talk about your favorite cartoons when you were a kid. Who was your all-time favorite cartoon character?

**Christmas Concert** During the Christmas season, check your newspapers for local concerts in churches, theaters, or orchestras, and plan a special night. Drive through town to see the Christmas lights before or after the event. Vote on which display is your favorite and revisit it another night. Make it an annual tradition.

**Coloring-Book Time** Get some coloring books and a big box of crayons with lots of colors. Select pictures for each other to color and have a contest. Feel free to color outside the lines and get creative with color selection. Display your favorite pictures on your refrigerator.

**Cupcake Party** Bake cupcakes together. After they're done, see how creative you can be in decorating them. Try using icing, sprinkles, nuts, or anything else you desire to decorate them. When you're finished, share them with a neighbor and help make their day.

**Dream Time** Spend an evening sharing your hopes and dreams for the future. Think ahead one year, five years, and the distant future. "What do you want to be (or do) if you ever grow up?" Don't let money influence you. This is a time to dream. Like a little boy once said, "If a guy ain't got a dream, how is he ever gonna make his dream come true."

**Dress-up Dinner Date** Dress to the nines, but eat dinner at home. After dinner, go to a nice restaurant for dessert and coffee. Pretend it's your anniversary. Spend some time just talking, sharing special moments in your marriage, and planning a special date in the future.

**Duck Time** Gather some leftover bread or some cups of birdseed, and head to a park or beach to feed the waterfowl. See how close you can get the birds to come to you, maybe even let them eat out of your hand. Then go and have lunch at your favorite place.

**Flowers** Find a local flower shop or even a supermarket, and buy some loose flowers. Then, go around the street and find strangers who look like they need a word of encouragement. Give them a flower and wish them the best. It might be so much fun you'll go back for more flowers or put it on your list to do again sometime.

**Fly Helicopters** Buy two helicopters from a toy store that you can fly around the house, or outside. Have fun seeing if you can make them fly alongside each other without crashing. Practice makes perfect.

**Friends Calling** List several friends you haven't talked with in a long time, maybe some old school friends or lonely relatives. Get on the speakerphone and do some catching up. This is not only fun but very meaningful to those you call. Take turns deciding whom to call and spread some cheer. Then pop some popcorn and reminisce.

**Funny Survey** Get some clipboards and dress like you are conducting an important survey in a public place. Ask strangers funny questions like how many times they brush their teeth in a day, what was the best thing they had to eat the day before, or what's the next car they would like to buy. Use your imagination and have fun.

**Garage Sales** Check the newspaper for garage sales, especially neighborhood sales, where everyone has their stash on display. Rummage through some of them to pick out a special treasure to give to your partner. You can set a dollar limit and have fun haggling to see which of you gets the most for your money. Then go out to breakfast or brunch and have fun with your newfound treasure. You could always add increments by starting with one dollar, then three dollars, and finally five dollars, with bragging rights included.

You might even find a real treasure that you both decide you just have to have for your house.

**Garden Magic** Go to a flower or garden show and enjoy the display. Many communities have some special gardens that come alive certain times of the year like azaleas, tulips, or flowering trees. Get some ideas for your garden and stop by a garden shop. Pick out a special rose bush or flowering plant, and go home and plant it.

**Go Camping** Find a local camping site and plan a campout. Borrow some equipment if need be, and don't forget a blow-up mattress. Make the simplest of meals; maybe you won't even choose to cook. But you may want to at least roast some marshmallows or hot dogs.

**Halloween Reversal** Get some candy and bags of goodies and head out in the neighborhood. Ring doorbells and say "Trick or Treat," and ask if any children live there. Give out the goodies, especially in neighborhoods where there are a lot of children. It works best if it is not Halloween. Just have fun with the kids.

**Have a Chat** Go to a public place and see how long you can get people to chat with you before they go on their way. Have a couple of interesting questions ready that are easy to answer. How long have you lived here? What do you like best about it? Where did you grow up? Can you recommend a good restaurant in the area? You might well turn a stranger into a newfound friend.

**Hobby Shop Project** Take a trip to your local hobby shop and pick out a project that you would enjoy working on together. Build something, like a rocket, or do a special craft project. It may even be something you will paint and use. The fun is in the doing, not necessarily in the result. Maybe each of you will pick your own project that you will work on together.

**Home Depot** Plan a date to Home Depot or Lowes and wander through the place, getting ideas for your home and some improvements. You can get great ideas from the bath and kitchen departments or from the gardening center. Beware of impulse buying, but come away with ideas for future activities or projects that you will both enjoy.

**Home Movie** Look around your house to find some odd clothing and props. Think up a funny scene to act out, get out your camera, and make the film. Each of you can take a turn at being the star.

**House Hunting** Go house hunting. Drive through some new neighborhoods and look for open house signs. Builders often have several models on display. Go in and take a look. Make note of what you liked and disliked, and see if any of these ideas may show up in your future. Choose your favorite room and why you like it.

**Just Ask Questions** Sit down and write out some bizarre or strange questions. Go to a neighborhood that is not your own, and knock on doors. Tell people you are conducting a special survey of public opinion and they have been selected. See how many people you can get to answer the questions. Thank them and tell them they have made an important contribution. If not a neighborhood, stop people on the street and ask a couple of questions. People might think you are from Candid Camera. Have fun with the different responses.

**Latte** Pick your favorite coffee shop and order your favorite beverage. Then just slow down and talk about life. Share some of your hopes and dreams, both personal and for your marriage.

**Lingerie Shopping** Go shopping for some lingerie together. Get something special and then go home and model it. Who know what this might lead to!

**Lunch Date** Eat lunch in the middle of a roundabout. Bring a blanket and a picnic basket and have fun. Watch people's faces as they circle you. Wave to the onlookers as if that was the perfect place for a picnic, and watch them shake their heads as they drive away. Maybe someone will even circle twice, trying to figure out what in the world you are doing.

**Make Kites** Go to a craft shop and buy some kite sticks and paper. Make a couple of kites with funny tails and go to an open space and fly them. See whose kite flies the best.

**Makeup Artists** Gather up a lot of makeup items, and take turns trying to make your partner look handsome or beautiful. Be creative! Then take pictures and show them to your friends to see who wins the title of the best makeup artist.

**Memory Lane** Get out the old photo albums and share pictures of you as a baby or growing up, and tell some of the stories behind the pictures. Laugh at what you looked like years ago; maybe you had funny glasses, a weird hairdo, or unflattering clothes. Fix a special drink or get one with two straws.

**Paint a Room** Go to the paint store and get everything you need to paint a room in your house. Choose the curtains or décor and make it a joint project. Put your creativity into your efforts to make it just what you want.

**Paint Your Own Pottery** Many towns have studios that provide bisque pottery for you to paint, and they will fire your creation for you. Otherwise check out hobby shops.

**People Bingo** Make a list of outrageous things that people might wear or carry. This might be clothing, hats, kids, purses, grocery items, or anything else you can think of. Then go to a Walmart or similar store, split up for a limited time, and see which of you can spot people wearing or carrying the objects. Check off each item and compare notes at a specific time. Loser has to buy the winner a hot fudge sundae at a nearby restaurant. Don't cheat!

**People Watching** Go to an airport, train station, or your local mall. Find a comfortable place to sit and just watch people. Make up stories about what they are doing there, where they are going, whom they will see, or what they are shopping for. Pick out the one who is happiest and the one who appears to be the saddest. Maybe you can even speak to someone who looks lonely and share some cheer. Then treat yourself to a special coffee or something to eat before you return home. If you are at an airport, maybe you can share where you would most like to go if you could or why you are glad you don't have to go anywhere.

**Petting Zoo** Go to a petting zoo and have fun with the animals. Pick out a favorite that you would adopt if you were to have a zoo in your backyard. Of course you will want to buy treats to feed the animals while you are there.

**Playdough Fun** Buy several cans of playdough and have a sculpture contest. See how many recognizable, creative things each of you can make in a period of twenty to thirty minutes. Use different colors. Then mix up the dough again and see if you can do better the second time.

**Play in the Rain** On a warm, rainy day, go out for a walk. Let it wash over you and enjoy getting wet. Maybe the song "Singing in the Rain" will come to mind, and you can try some new dance steps. Of course you can always take umbrellas if you don't want to get wet.

**Progressive Dinner** Create your own progressive dinner. Go to four different restaurants: one for an appetizer, another for a salad, then for an entree, and finally one for a dessert. You could do this for little cost by picking all fast-food restaurants, or choose a fancy restaurant for dessert.

**Project Time** Work on a fun project together. Buy supplies, figure out the instructions, and get to work! There is no limit to the ideas you can find. If you need ideas, go to a home and garden center and pick up one of their books of ideas, as well as the materials you need to create your project.

**Puzzles Anyone?** Go to a store that sells puzzles. Pick out one that you both like and start to work on it. It may take days, even weeks, but as you work together to finish it, spend the time sharing thoughts and dreams. You could always have a ten-minute contest to see which of you can find the most pieces that fit together within that time.

**Rent a Convertible** Rent a convertible on a beautiful night, drive to the nearest drive-in movie theater, and pretend you are teenagers again. Take the long way home, and be sure to share a special goodnight kiss.

**Road to Nowhere** Get in the car with no plans. Start driving and see where the road leads you. Enjoy the journey as you play some of your favorite music. Don't go home until you feel like it.

**Roof-Top Picnic** Find a place where you can go up on a roof and have a picnic. See things you have never seen before. Pretend you are kings for the day and observe all that is below you.

**Rose Delight** Plan ahead. Go to a restaurant early, and ask the waiter to bring a rose to your spouse each time he or she visits the table when you dine there that evening.

**Shop for Cars** Go to the place where all the auto sales centers are located, and check out all the latest modes and features. Make sure they know you are just looking and not ready to buy yet; maybe even leave your wallets and credit cards home so you won't be tempted. Check several different places, and pick out the car of your dreams. You might even take a test drive just for fun.

**Skipping Rocks** Find some flat rocks for skipping, and buy some glow sticks at a craft store. Put the rocks in a plastic bag, break the glow sticks open, and pour them into the bag with the rocks. Go to a lake at night, and skip the glowing rocks across the water. Then go out for a cup of hot chocolate and a favorite dessert.

**Something New** Teach the other how to do something they've never tried. This can be anything, from learning to play the guitar to a new card game. It could be how to make an apple pie, or how to play a new computer game.

**Store Time** Go to a store like Rooms to Go or Ikea, any store that has a variety of room settings will work. Wander around and pick out your favorite rooms. You can make up a story for each room. What do you think would be happening in each room? What would you like to see happening if it were your room?

**Tea Time** Go to a fancy hotel in time for afternoon tea. Dress appropriately, of course. Enjoy the time together by pretending you are in a foreign country, perhaps even talk to each other in accents. If you are not up for tea, you can always substitute with wine and cheese or a cup of special coffee.

**Try Some Art** Take an art class together at a local recreation center or community college. Too expensive? Grab two canvases and some paints and get to work. You may even create some pretty amazing artwork for your home. If you aren't the artistic types, you can always start with something more instructional (like a Paint-by-Numbers kit) as you begin your career. Otherwise, just have fun.

**Wii Olympics** Get out your Wii Sports and begin a competition in bowling, batting, tennis, or whichever sport you choose. Or, if you have the fitness program, pretend you are going to the gym together and get fit. This is also a great idea for a group date; gather several couples and have a competition using Wii Sports.

# Romantic Dates

What makes a date romantic? Is it the setting, the atmosphere, the elegance of the place, the cost, or an indefinable quality? While some settings are obviously more romantic than others, romance is not the same for everyone. What makes a man feel romantic is different from what makes a woman feel romantic. The bottom line is often a matter of desire. How do we make our partner feel desired? What makes our partner feel beautiful or handsome or sought after? What do we say to each other to make our partner feel valued and special? Any date can be romantic if we make it that way. You can be in a romantic place and have a miserable time if you choose to criticize and complain. The atmosphere may help to bring out the romantic in you, but it is really a matter of the heart. Are you connecting deeply with feelings of love? Choose a setting that adds to the romance: the candles, the music, the beauty, and so on. But putting that special romantic touch on it is what makes it truly memorable.

**ABC's** Light some candles, pour something to drink, add some music, and sit down with a paper and pencil and write the alphabet down the page. Then fill in something for each letter that you love about your partner, and exchange your ABC's. This can be a great affirmation of each other and a paper you will want to save.

**Antique Hunting** Get a list of antique stores in your area and begin a tour. Look for a real bargain, but make an agreement before you tour whether you are shopping for something special or just having fun looking. See which one of you can find the best treasure.

**Boating** Find a park that has paddleboats, and rent one for an hour or so. Take along some snacks or even a picnic lunch. Paddle some, rest some, eat some, talk some, and make it an experience to remember. Enjoy the ducks, the frogs, the turtles, or whatever wildlife you find in the lake or pond.

**Breakfast in Bed** Plan a special morning where you can spend some time in bed. Prepare for breakfast the night before, so it can be easy to serve the next morning. Add some soft music, some books or magazines to read, and simply enjoy the moment.

**Candlelight and Chocolate** Plan an evening for candlelight and chocolate. Find some recipes for chocolate fudge, chocolate-covered nuts, and other chocolate goodies. Have fun making things, tasting them, and finally, prepare a plate or two to take to a lonely neighbor or surprise a friend.

**Candlelight Picnic** Have a candlelight picnic in your backyard. Plan something special for food, and spend some time sharing some of your favorite memories with each other. Hopefully you won't need any mosquito repellant, but be prepared just in case.

**Christmas Lights** Find a neighborhood where there is a decorating contest. Drive there, get out of the car, walk through the neighborhood holding hands, and pretend you have come to judge the contest. Pick out the winner. You could always write a note to tuck in their door saying you have voted them the best. Otherwise, just enjoy the walk and the fun of doing this together.

**Cooking Together** You can plan a special night for cooking together. Decide on the menu, and go shopping together to get whatever you need. Go home and let the fun begin. If you aren't both experienced cooks, you will have some fun teaching the fine art of boiling water or holding a knife. No criticism, just fun! Once all the dishes are prepared, make sure the table is set with candles and flowers. Have fun sharing the experience, and plan a different menu for the next time.

**Couples Massage** Find a massage parlor that provides a couples massage side-by-side at the same time. Enjoy the aroma, the soft touch, and some more serious touch to loosen up those muscles. Have the fun of doing it together and sharing in the experience.

**Cozy Night** Read a book together beside the fire. Take turns reading to each other. Get creative by using special effects or acting out the scene. Make it fun and romantic by using your imagination.

**Dance the Night Away** Few things can be much more romantic than finding a special hotel, club, or restaurant that has a great dance band. Hopefully they will play some of your favorites, as well as some slow dances for cheek to cheek. Order a special beverage, and share romantic memories between dances.

**Dinner Cruise** Many places on the water have a cruise boat that offers dinner cruises. Get a reservation and plan a special evening for dinner, water views, and hopefully a sunset. There is no way this can't be a romantic evening out and certainly one to remember.

**Dream Home** Get some graph paper or drawing paper and begin to design your dream house together. Decide on style and curb appeal. Draw each room and decide what goes in it, what color the paint would be, and what amenities would be included. Make sure you create a special place for each of you, like a garage workshop, a movie room, or special bath and shower.

**Dress Up for Dinner** Play dress-up for dinner but order take-out food. Wear your classiest and most sophisticated dinner clothes and have a candlelit dinner at your home, probably with a romantic CD playing in the background. Dim the lights and invite your sweetheart to a slow dance. The purpose of the takeout food is to give a little twist to the date experience. But if you're planning to go all out, you can cook a fantastic dinner together.

**Fantasy Date** Sit down together with some paper and each of you write down your idea of a fantasy date—one that you would think might be the most special date of all. Share your ideas with each other, and then see if you can combine some of the ideas to make it the most special date of the year—one to remember. You may have enough ideas for several special dates.

**Fast-Food Romance** The next time you and your spouse dine under the golden arches, bring a tablecloth and a candle. This bold move shows off your creativity and adds an element of fun and romance to your otherwise ordinary date.

**Fire Pot** Get a fire pot for your deck or patio if you don't have one. Then sit out at night and enjoy the fire. It might be a great time to roast hot dogs or marshmallows, and share some great memories. You may need some mosquito repellant, but don't let that spoil the moment.

**First Date** Go on a second first date. Get dressed up, drive separately to a secret place, and pretend you've just met.

Hold hands. Ask questions awkwardly. Get butterflies. Maybe even a first kiss? See if you can discover something new about each other that you never knew before.

**First Times** Take your partner back to the place where you two first met, first kissed, or any other kind of first. To make the event more memorable and interesting, take along a video camera or phone and make a mini movie with you recreating this first.

**Five Wishes** Take some time to write down five wishes you would like to have your partner fulfill. Make the requests reasonable. Then share your list with your partner, and each of you choose three wishes from the list that you will endeavor to fulfill. Make each one special.

**Flirty, Fun Park Romance** Book the baby-sitter now: you're taking your spouse to the amusement park! Especially at night with the lights aglow, family-fun parks can be a perfect place for a summer date. For romance with a view, snuggle up on a fairground classic, the Ferris wheel. For greater thrills, brave the roller coasters together! Spark up your old, flirty ways while chasing each other in bumper cars, riding the merry-go-round, and laughing your way through the house of mirrors. And don't forget the cotton candy, mini-donuts, Whack-A-Mole, and the impossible to win stuffed prizes. With this much fun, you might not want to tell the kids where you're going!

**Four Gifts and Food** Go shopping for four inexpensive gifts that symbolize or express love for your partner. Then plan a cheap restaurant tour to some fast-food restaurants. Get an appetizer at one, a salad at the next, then a main item like a burger, hot dog, or sandwich, and finally a dessert at the fourth one. Give each other a simple gift at each restaurant, and spend time together. Don't hurry. Of course you can always spend more and pick different restaurants, but it is just as romantic to share your love in less-expensive ways.

**Hold Hands** Walk hand in hand along any kind of water—river, lake, or ocean. Throw in a sunset for the perfect romantic moment. Share some special feelings, or memories, as you make it a memorable time.

**Horse-Drawn Buggy** Many towns have historic districts where you can get a tour through the area in a horse-drawn buggy. Wrap up in a blanket if it's cold, and enjoy the trip through history. Check out some of the older homes and places of interest. Then go for coffee and share what you enjoyed most. Hopefully, it will be "just being together."

**Ice-skating** If it's wintertime, go to your local ice-skating rink and have a skate date. You may have to hold each other up. If you are experienced, try some ice dancing together. Then go and get some hot chocolate.

**Leaf Peeping** Check the Internet to find out when the leaves will be in full color on a mountain or hillside near you. A skyline drive or parkway are great choices. Play some soft music as you drive slowly through the winding roads. Stop along the way to take pictures of each other, or ask someone to take pictures of you both. Find a quaint place along the road to stop for lunch, or simply buy some of your favorite donuts to take along with your coffee.

**Library Fun** Go to the local library and read books of interest to each other. Try reading poetry together. Find a children's book you used to love or read to your children, and read it to each other. Mimic the animals, sounds, and faces. Do it quietly, maybe in whispers, or you may get fussed at. Check out a favorite book or movie and take it home to share later.

**Love Cards** Go to a card shop and pick out seven cards that express love in different ways, avoiding the obvious birthday and anniversary cards. Pick a card that expresses your love for your partner, and give one to your partner every day for a week. See the impact this kind of repeating-love theme has on your relationship.

**Luau** Go to a music store and get some island music. Decorate your living room with island décor. Plan a menu from island specials, and have a great luau right in your own home. You might even want to share this experience with some of your friends.

**Massage**? Get some candles to light, some warm lotion, and whatever else might feel good, and take turns giving each other a massage. Turn on some soft, romantic music. Who knows where this could lead?

**Meteor Shower** Stargazing can always be fun. However, nothing beats a meteor shower, where stars fall like rain. Lie on a blanket and wish on the shooting stars. Share some with your partner, but always keep one special wish a secret. Maybe you will tell your partner later, or just keep him or her guessing.

**Midnight Swim** On a warm night, maybe in the moonlight, go for a midnight swim in your pool or a nearby lake or beach. It might even be a good time for skinny-dipping, or just a time to enjoy something you don't do every night.

**Movie Special** Pick a romantic movie you would both like to see. After the movie, make it an extra-special occasion by going out for ice cream. Go all out and get a sundae of several different flavors and a multitude of toppings. Find a place to sit, and share your favorite parts of the movie. Do not count calories, just indulge.

**Nature Walk** Go to a beautiful park and take a nature walk hand in hand. Notice special plants, flowers, or trees. See how many birds you can name. Share some new thoughts and feelings about being together. Pick a trail that ends in something special and romantic, like a cascading waterfall.

**New Shopping Mall** Go to a new shopping mall, one you have never been to before. Do some window-shopping for starters. Check out the shops and see if any of your favorites are there. Take your time and explore; you may even find a new favorite. Try to find a special place to eat besides a food court. Pick out a small gift for each other, and just have fun.

**Night Drive** Go for a night drive. Pack up some good tunes and ride off into the sunset.

**Pennies for Dreams** Get a roll of pennies from the bank and find a fountain or wishing well. Take turns tossing in a penny as you share a hope, dream, or wish. See if you can use all of the pennies before you run out of dreams. If not, start taking turns sharing things you like or admire in each other and affirm that as you toss in your penny. You can always choose what you want to share as you toss your next penny.

**A Picnic Full of Memories** This year, treat your valentine to a carpet picnic...in your living room! Instead of making an extravagant meal, separately buy each other's favorite appetizers and finger foods. Try to pick foods that hold certain memories about them—like a flavor you had on your first date, or the time your wife was pregnant and craved only salt and vinegar chips. At home, serve the items on little plates on a blanket on the floor. Light candles while you dine, turn on some music, and share memories of your life together according to the food you bought!

**Picnic on the Beach** Set up a picnic on the beach and watch the sun set or rise together. Try picking a place you have never been before, but be sure to check it out in advance. Make it a time to share something special. Snuggle up together! Make others around think you are newlyweds.

**Play Pool** Find a local pool hall or game room where there is a pool table. If you don't know how to play, get your date to teach you. This act can be extremely romantic.

**Play Your Song** Put on the CD that has your special song and dance around the room as you share the memories. Make it a plan that whenever that song is played you will dance to the music.

**Remember When** Spend an evening completing the sentence that starts with, "Remember when . . ." Go from one memory to another as far back as you can remember. Remember what it was like at the beginning of your courtship, or marriage. Remember how you used to do some things together, even wash and dry dishes before you got your first dishwasher. Remember what it was like before cell phones, when you actually talked to each other without texting.

**Renew Your Vows** Choose a special anniversary and plan to recreate your wedding. If you didn't write your own vows in your wedding, write them for the renewal. Let them express the years you have shared together. Invite a few special guests, and make it a moment to remember.

**Rent a Limo** Renting a limo can make any date romantic and exciting as you watch it pull up in front of the house just for you. It may be a special party, the theater, or a trip to the airport as you leave for a vacation to the islands.

**Road Trip** Go on a road trip for the day. Map out the route, stop at anything fun on the way, and listen to special music as you drive. Better yet, rent a convertible on a nice day and drive along a lake, beach, or pretty country road. Get your scarf and beanie, and pretend you are famous. Plan to return in the moonlight.

**Role Reversal** Plan a date where you try to reverse roles. Let her open the car doors and maybe even pick up the check. Let him follow her lead and be treated like a lady. Try to imitate each other's mannerisms, habits, and favorite poses. See how well you know each other as you act this out in fun. Laugh with and at each other as you try to stay in character as each other.

**Romantic Movie Night** Rent or download your favorite romantic movie. Pop some popcorn and don't forget to snuggle together. Hold hands during the teary parts, and whisper some sweet nothings in each other's ears.

**Scavenger Hunt** Set up a scavenger hunt for your partner. Be creative with the clues. You might hide them in roses you leave at certain places or with people who have touched you both as a couple. You can make it a little easier by placing the clues all over your house. If you want to make it a genuine hunt, plan ahead and put the clues in special places around your town. And of course, the final prize is you.

**Scrapbook Time** Get out some old photos or memorabilia you have been saving and create a scrapbook. You could even cut out some pictures from magazines of vacation spots you have visited or things you have done together to add. Leave space at the end and continue to add to it as you find other things to include. Then share your experiences as you go along or when you look through it once you're finished.

**Seasonal Festivals** Go to seasonal festivals, for example a strawberry festival. Enjoy picking strawberries and do something special with the ones you take home. Try strawberries and cream, or try your hand at baking a short cake. If strawberries aren't your favorite, pick peaches together and make a pie. Or try your luck at a local fish fry or a food-tasting event. The possibilities are endless, and you can tailor your choices to fit your tastes.

**Shower Together** Every now and then, take a shower together. Enjoy washing each other's bodies and sharing some tender moments. It may be before a special date, or it may just be a special act of love. It could become a habit that you will continue through the years. You can always dim the lights, or light some candles, and make it even more romantic.

**Story Time** Remember how you first met? Share your spouse's perspective. Write the story from your point of view and have your spouse do the same, then share your stories with each other. Enter them in your computer, and save them to review from time to time.

**Sunrise** Get up before dawn and head for the beach or an open place where you can experience a sunrise together. While you are waiting for the sun to rise, talk about your future and even plan or daydream about your next vacation together. Then go out for breakfast!

**Surprise Date** During the week before the date, ask your partner a series of questions, without explanation. "Red or yellow?" could determine the color of the flowers you would get. "Fast or slow?" might decide whether the date is at a fast-food or sit-down restaurant. "Hot or cold?" might mean the kind of special coffee or drink. Think up several more pairs of alternatives depending on the date you have in mind. Then on the date night, tell her you are going to surprise her with a date where she has already made all the decisions in advance, and let her experience the fun of each decision she made.

**Sweet Stuff** Get out the whip cream, chocolate sauce, nuts, and other fixings, and see what kind of sundaes you can create and enjoy. Don't count the calories, just have fun.

**Time Capsule** Create a time capsule that contains your dreams for the next ten years. Bury it or hide it away. Then open it ten years later and see how many of those dreams have come true. Celebrate each dream that has become a reality and make some new ones for the next ten years.

**Travel Agency** Visit a travel agency and inquire about special trips that might be available. Gather some brochures, pictures, and information. Go home, cut out pictures and paste them on a board until the day when that trip becomes a reality.

**You Have Mail** Write a series of love letters, each one sharing something different you appreciate about your mate. Make each one different as you focus on another aspect of your love. Mail them three days apart, so your partner will be surprised on days when this special mail arrives. Let the last one be an invitation to a romantic date.

**Vision Board** Create a marriage "vision board" for the next year. Grab lots of magazines and newspapers from friends the week prior, and spend the night listening to your favorite songs while cutting and pasting your dreams together. Hang it up in your kitchen and watch your dreams come true as the year unfolds.

**Walking and Talking** This is a simple date that can be very special. Pick a place to walk. It could be in a mall, on a track, in the woods, by the shore, or around the neighborhood. Make it a time to simply talk with each other—no phones or technology—just talk. The more positive the conversation, the more fun it will be. And it will be good exercise.

**Walmart Fun** Go to Walmart in the middle of the night, and play with all of the toys you can find. Pretend you are kids, and enjoy all the new and different toys, especially those you never had an opportunity to play with. Remember some of your favorite toys and share stories. You might even pick up a couple of toys to give to less-fortunate children, especially during the Christmas season.

**Waterfalls** If you live in a mountain area, or can drive to one, tour the waterfalls. Get a map that shows where they are and how far the hike is to see them. Go to several, if possible, and make sure to pack a picnic lunch to eat beside your favorite. Enjoy the scenery on the way, and take lots of pictures. Pick a name for each waterfall that you visit, maybe related to what you did there. Wear (or bring) your swimsuits in case you want to take a dip or slide down the waterfall. Check out the plants and flowers you might see on the way back.

**Window-Shopping** Go to a ritzy part of town after dark and walk up and down the streets to window-shop. This is especially fun during the Christmas season, where there are many special lights and decorations. Pick out the winning window; the place you would love to go in if the store was still open. Maybe plan a trip back during the daytime.

**<u>Write a Love Letter</u>** Dedicate it to the other person ten years from now. Read them to each other then lock them away for safekeeping. That should make for a fun date night in ten years. You could always choose a different timeframe; it's all up to you.

**<u>Write a Poem</u>** Spend some time thinking special thoughts about your special person, and then write them a poem. It doesn't have to be a great poem and it doesn't have to rhyme. It just has to have some special words of love for your partner. Then, plan a date in a quiet place, and read your poem to your partner. No matter what the poem is like, it will be a keeper.

# Outdoor / Active Dates

When it comes to romance, a lot of guys find it very romantic to have a date with a playmate. It makes a guy feel special to have a woman who enjoys active dates with him. Women may find active dates romantic, as well. Whether it is romantic or not, active dates can be a lot of fun for both of you. Here are a number of simple activities that can be as much fun as you want them to be.

**Ball Game** Go to a game hosted by your local high school or college. Pick a sport you both enjoy, or introduce your partner to something new. Perhaps you'll find a new mutual interest.

**Basketball** Grab a basketball and find your local basketball court. Play a game of horse, around the world, or one-on-one.

**Batting Cage** Try your skill at a batting cage. Set the speed so you can hit the ball with some regularity. Teach each other how to bat. If you really want a challenge, reverse the way you usually bat; if you usually bat right-handed, try your left. Learning how to hold the bat can be fun in itself.

**Bike Ride** Take an early morning or evening bike ride together. Explore your neighborhood or the countryside. Stop at a quaint café for breakfast or get an ice cream cone along the way. In fact, stop whenever you feel the urge. It's not a race, it's a journey.

**Bird Watching** Get a book that describes the birds of America and study some of the birds that are common in your region. Then head for the woods and see how many different birds you can identify. If you get a bird bath and some feeders you may be surprised at how many different birds come to you in a week, month, or through the changing seasons.

**Boating** Get out your boat, or rent one on a beautiful day, and explore a new river or cove. Pack a lunch to eat on the water or stop at a restaurant where you can dock for a snack. Don't forget the sunscreen. Be adventurous! Check out the wildlife on the way home.

**Bowling** Take your partner to a late-night bowling alley, and enjoy the game, music, lights, people, and fun. Forget the score! Count only gutter balls or just strikes or just splits. If you are good bowlers, then make a competition of it where the winner buys the refreshments afterward. Watch the other bowlers and guess who might get a strike first.

**Camping Out** Take a romantic camping trip together. It can be for one night, a long weekend, or a week if you prefer. If you don't own a tent and blow-up mattress, see if you can find someone to loan them to you. Try your hand at cooking over an open fire, even if you're just roasting hotdogs and marshmallows. Don't forget the mosquito repellant.

**Canoeing** Go canoeing or kayaking on a lake or slow river. There are some beautiful places you can explore. Pick a wildlife reserve for additional fun.

**Croquet** Get an old-fashioned croquet set and play a few rounds. You could always add some other people if you are so inclined. If the course is bumpy so you miss an easy shot, all the more fun. Your ball might even just jump over the ball you are sure you can hit.

**Dancing** Dancing is always a fun and romantic activity, but take it to the next level by dancing in an unusual place. For example, find a dock jutting into the water, use your phone to play music, and dance on the dock. Just be careful that you don't end up in the water when you twirl, or maybe that would just add to the fun.

**Dog Walking** Take your dog(s) out for a walk in a new place, or find a doggie park where they can play. You can spend your time talking about your favorite dates, and plan to have another of your favorites soon.

**Favorite Sport** Choose a sport you both enjoy and go play together. Almost any sport can be fun when you do it together. The list of sports is almost endless, so this could be a series of dates.

**Fishing** There are all kinds of ways to fish. You could do some casting in a local pond or the old-fashioned bobber fishing on a cane pole. You could rent a boat or head out on a fishing boat with a captain, who will guarantee that you will catch fish. Even if you didn't catch anything, you can have some great conversation.

**Fountains** Map out all of the fountains in your area, and make an afternoon of finding them and admiring their beauty. You can always toss coins in the fountains, and make wishes that you can share with each other.

**Frisbee** Go to the park and play a game of Frisbee. (Maybe take along your dog if he likes to play.)

**Gardening** Go dig in the dirt and plant something together. You could stop at a garden shop to buy some plants, or prepare a bed for seeds and plant a vegetable garden. Then have some fun as you water and weed, and enjoy the fruits of your hard labor at harvest time when you pick some luscious, ripe tomatoes.

**Glow Sticks** Go to a toy store and get some glow sticks. Then go to a park at night and make some glowing images. Lose all restraint, and pretend you are kids again.

**Go-Karts** Find an arcade that has go-karts or bumper cars. Have fun chasing each other, bumping each other, or whatever inspires you in the moment.

**Golfing** Sometimes golfing can be fun. It all depends on your attitude, not just how well you play. Some people make every golf outing an unhappy event—they don't play as well as they wanted to. When you golf as a couple (unless you are great golfers), why not throw away the score card, and just enjoy the great scenery and have fun with every shot. The more shots, the more you get for your money, so have at it.

**Hiking** Go on a hike with a picnic basket full of goodies for you and your date to share whenever you find a nice place to stop. Enjoy the beauty of God's creation together. Conclude your journey with back and foot rubs.

**Horseback Riding** Find a stable nearby that has horses you can ride. See if there is a picturesque trail ride that you can share. Maybe a guide will take you someplace special. Otherwise just have fun sharing the time together.

**Ice-skating** Maybe you haven't been ice-skating in years. Grab your skates, and head for the local ice skating rink. Don't have skates? You can rent them. It might even be more fun if you can find a frozen pond nearby where the local kids go to skate, and you can be one of the kids again.

**Jogging** Jogging can be a good way to spend some time together. Pick a pace that you both enjoy. The beauty of the path you are on will only enhance the fun. Of course, you could always have a short race to the end. Think of creative ways to cool down.

**Learn Racquetball** If you want some action, try your hand at racquetball. It is a fun game for the energetic, and you can get in better shape by playing it on a regular basis.

**Mud Fight** Find a muddy area, dress in old clothing, and have a mud fight. Try to find a place where mud races are held, go through an obstacle course, and see who comes up with the least mud. There may be a hose where you can have a water fight to get cleaned up afterward.

**Nighttime Walk** Water and moonlight can be romantic. Is there a lake, river, or fountain near your home? Take a walk along a body of water at night. Pause and gaze at the light shimmering on the water. Dream and imagine together.

**Paddleboats** Rent a paddleboat and paddle away on your local lake, park, or wherever they have self-propelled boats. Add a picnic lunch you can eat when you are resting your legs.

**Picking Stars** Find the high point in your town where you can view the lights of the city or where you can see the stars really well. Pick a special star and name it for your loved one. If you really like astronomy, there are actually places where you can pay to name a star and make it official. A creative date and present all-in-one!

**Picnic** Try an old-fashioned picnic in a secluded spot. Lay out a tablecloth and snacks. Some wine might be a nice touch. Perhaps read some romantic poetry to each other. It need not be original, just something you took the effort to find.

**Picture Taking** Pick out some special places in your town and go take some pictures. Maybe you can choose some special places from your childhood if you grew up there, or places that hold meaning for you as a couple. Or you might just visit some new places and explore. Then share your picture show.

**Racing Cars** Purchase some cheap, remote-control cars. Take them to the park and have a race. Reward the winner appropriately (you decide what).

**Rain Dancing** Grab a boom box or phone that plays music, and go out in the rain for some dancing. Raincoats optional. Of course you will want to sing along. Afterward, go in and dry each other off.

**Ride Motorcycles** You may own motorcycles or just borrow them for a special ride. There is nothing like feeling the air blowing in your face with your scarf flying behind you. There are so many paths and trails where you can take a motorcycle that you can't take a car. If a motorcycle proves too challenging, try a motor scooter.

**Rock-Climbing** See if any of the gyms or recreational facilities in your area have rock-climbing walls. See if you can trust each other with the safety ropes, and maybe have a race to the top. If you're an experienced climber, take your gear to a state park and get climbing. Plan something special once you reach the top._

**Rollerblading** Get some rollerblades, and head for a safe place to skate. Be sure to bring your pads and helmet so you won't get hurt if you fall. You can also go to a roller-skating rink and rent some skates. Try some dancing together as you learn to skate backward or even twirl.

**Sand Castle** Head for the beach with buckets and shovels to make some sand castles. Pick any kind of object to create. Sculpt objects on the beach and see if you can get some people on the beach to become judges. Whoever has the winning object will be the guest of the other for lunch or supper. Then take a dip in the water to cool off and have fun. Don't forget the camera to take some pictures.

**Scuba Diving** Take some lessons to get certified. Find a beautiful place to go deeper once you are prepared.

**Silly Stuff** Do something silly that reminds you of your childhood. Climb a tree together, catch lightning bugs, or feed some ducks.

**Skydiving** This is not for the faint of heart, but can be an exciting date. Think how much fun it would be to jump out of an airplane and drift quietly to land (minus any screams, of course). It can be a memorable date—one you will talk about for years afterward.

**Skiing** When you go to a ski resort and learn to ski, you can have all kinds of fun, starting on the bunny trails and moving up to ones that are more difficult. You may need some lessons, or you may be experts. Either way it can be a great time of winter fun.

**Sledding** Get out the sleds or toboggans after a snow, and head for the hills. See if you can both fit on a sled or toboggan and slide down the hill. You could always race back to the top if you are in the shape to do it.

**Snorkeling** Go to a beach or even a lake, take your snorkeling gear, and see what you can discover. Of course, there are some islands that have clear water over reefs that provide some fantastic snorkeling, if you can just get there. If you are a snorkeling enthusiast, it's a must-do.

**Square Dancing** Dress up in your best country outfits and find a square dance. Twirl and do-si-do the night away. Don't know how? Take some lessons. Even if you don't get all the steps right, it will still be fun.

**Sunrise/Sunset** Find a special place to watch the sunrise or sunset. If it is early morning at the beach, take some coffee and your favorite donuts while you wait, and maybe a blanket if it is a cool morning. Then go out for a special breakfast afterward. Do the same thing on another date, but make it a sunset.

**Take Salsa Lessons** Check with your local community center and see if they offer salsa lessons (or perhaps another dance you've always wanted to learn). Sign up and begin the fun. Once the lessons are over, you will have a new dating skill that you can use over and over for even more fun.

**Tandem Bikes** Go for a bike ride in your neighborhood. See if you can find a tandem bicycle to borrow or rent, so you can be even closer to your partner.

**Tennis, Anyone?** Playing tennis together can be a date that provides both exercise and some friendly competition. If you haven't played that much, it can still be fun if you don't take it too seriously. Swing with abandonment, and just have a good time doing it together.

**Try Your Luck** Go to a clover patch, and start hunting for some four-leaf clovers. If you find one, make a special wish for your partner. Maybe even sing "I'm Looking Over a Four-Leafed Clover" to your partner.

**Tubing** Find giant inner tubes and float down a lazy river. There are many places where you can rent tubes, and they'll even drop you off and pick you up. Watch out for unexpected rocks or larger rapids.

**Water Balloon Fight** Fill some small balloons with water, and have some fun being kids as you throw and duck and see if you can actually stay dry. Not likely, but grab a towel and have fun.

**Water Park** Find out if there are any water parks in your area and go try out the big slide. Splash each other and play like kids. If the kids around you are having more fun that you are, you are taking it too seriously.

**Water Ski** If you have a ski boat, you already know how much fun this can be. If you don't know how, learning can be fun, especially once you get up on the skis. Find a friend who has a ski boat and head for a lake where you can try it out.

**Workout** Join a local gym or exercise facility and start working out together. Turn your fat into muscle and enjoy the new you. Buy something new to wear to celebrate your progress.

# Educational Dates

Not all dating has to revolve around fun. Some great dates can be those where you learn something together. There are many educational opportunities that, when taken together, can be special dates. This is especially true when you learn something that you can continue to do together after the classes are over.

**Art Classes** You don't have to be a gifted artist to enjoy taking a class on painting. As you do it together, you can have fun sharing what you paint and choose which painting goes on your refrigerator.

**Adult Education** Check out the adult education classes that are available in your area or at your community center. Choose one that you can take together and both enjoy. It could range from developing a new technical skill to painting, from learning about local history to weight loss. You're bound to find something that will be of interest. This can be a fun and inexpensive date-night activity that involves a series of dates.

**Bible Study** Plan to do a Bible study together. It could be in a group through your church, or the two of you could get some help through the Internet or Bible study guides to have a one-on-one study. See what you can learn that might well enrich your marriage.

**Book Clubs** Join a local book club. You can enjoy reading and discussing the book together, and then join with others to see what they can contribute as well. You may be able to suggest a special book they will all enjoy.

**College Class** Check out the courses that are offered at your local community college. You may want to take a course together for credit, or choose one of interest you can audit.

**Computer Training** Want to learn how to use Microsoft Office? Find a company that offers training and join in a class together.

**Cooking Class** See if a local recreation center or a community college offers cooking classes. Go together and learn the art of cooking, and then go home and practice what you have learned. If you have a friend who loves to cook, see if they will give you a private lesson. This can be a lot of fun. Once you have cooked something special, enjoy it by candlelight.

**Dance Studio** Check out the local Fred Astaire dance studio and sign up for some lessons. You could be beginners, or up for some advanced steps.

**Financial Management** One of the best ways to get your finances under control is to take a course on financial management. Many churches offer a Dave Ramsey course that can make a major difference in how you approach and manage your money.

**Genealogy** Get on your computer and look up one of the sites that can help you find all of your ancestors. Find out where each of you came from and as much information about your family background as you can discover. This might lead to a trip to visit some relative you didn't even know you had.

**Guided Tour** Take a guided tour of a nearby city or your own that you have never taken before. Often we can live in a place and still miss what our city has to offer. It might even be a self-guided tour with headsets or other information that can lead you to the special sites.

**Historical Building** Go to the historical registry for your area and learn about the historical buildings in your city. Pick out a couple of them and spend a morning or afternoon visiting them and learning the history behind them.

**Hobbies** Start a new hobby together. Go to a bookstore to do some research. For example, if it is photography, check out information on cameras, lenses, and techniques. Buy a book on photography. Then go to a photo shop to get further information, and start taking some professional-looking pictures you can share with friends or on Facebook.

**Lessons** Decide to take some lessons together. They could be for a sport, like golf or tennis, or just something you've always wanted to do, like boating lessons or horseback riding. You can really enrich your marriage when you learn some new things together that you can use over a lifetime.

**Marriage Retreats** Check your church or local community for any marriage courses or retreats that you can attend together. There may be a book you read in advance and then share with a group, or just a series of sessions where you can gain some skill in communicating or resolving differences.

**Massage Class** Find a place that provides training in massage therapy, and see if they have a class for couples. Then get some training in massage and practice it at home with each other. Candlelight might be a nice touch.

**Museum** There are bound to be several museums in your community or nearby, like science or history museums. Check out what might be available, and then plan a date to go and investigate what they have to offer. You will learn some new things and enrich your understanding, which you can share with each other.

**National Parks** Find the location of a national park in your area and visit. Some have films you can watch or people who can give you a guided tour. Some are amazing in beauty, others in historical significance. You may need to make this an overnighter, which will only add to the fun.

**Planetarium** Visit a local planetarium. If you don't have one where you live, find out if there is one in a nearby city that you could plan to visit. Make it a special outing that you will both enjoy.

**Public Lectures** Check with your local newspaper to see what kinds of public lectures are available. These will change from week to week. Find one of interest to you and go. Then you can discuss what you learned, and plan your next one.

**Tourist Class** Some cities have a program in the off-season where you can be a tourist in your own city. You can get special rates to visit tourist attractions, as well as things like hotels or tickets to the theater. Go and explore what visitors pay to see. Stop and enjoy the things you may have passed by numerous times but have never experienced.

# Faith Building or Service Dates

There are many ways you can turn a date into a faith-building experience or simply an opportunity to engage in a service project in your community. These dates are especially important, as they help to build the foundation of your marriage and encourage you to explore the gift of serving, which is so essential in a good marriage. Husbands and wives are to be servants to each other, outdoing one another in acts of kindness. When couples extend this serving to others, it provides some real fulfillment.

**Animal Shelter** Volunteer at your local animal shelter. Better yet, help with a campaign to find homes for the animals (but not all at your home). Enjoy the moments you share together, and see if you can make a difference.

**Bake Cookies** Spend some time baking cookies or preparing plates of goodies that you can take to your neighbors, just because. A neighbor who has children would be especially fun. It doesn't need to be Christmas or a special time of the year. Just doing it makes it a special date to share with others.

**Bible Study Group** Join a Bible study group at your church or start one in your neighborhood. Spend some time sharing your favorite scriptures, or begin a study of one of the New Testament books. Ephesians is a good one for this purpose because it will help you learn how to relate to each other and how to improve your marriage.

**Caroling** Find some friends and go caroling through your neighborhood during the Christmas season. Then get together for some hot chocolate and sharing after you have finished your rounds. Or, go to a nursing home or senior-living facility and sing there. Just spread the joy.

**Christmas Family** There are usually a number of places (churches and restaurants, for example) that decorate their Christmas trees with pictures of families in need. Choose a family, buy some gifts for them, and deliver them personally for a special and rewarding experience.

**Church Outreach** Sign up to serve as a couple in an outreach program of your church, extend the love of Christ to others, and rekindle your love for one another.

**Church Worship** Go to your church services together, and share your experience as you have lunch together afterward. What was most meaningful to you? How can you best respond?

**Community Event** Look through your newspaper, and find some upcoming community events. Pick one, inquire how you can help, and make it a special date. This kind of activity will make your marriage even stronger.

**Encouragement** Visit a mutual friend or church family that needs some special encouragement. Take a meal to them at a time of a loss or just some words of affirmation. Keep them in your prayers.

**Fish Fry** During Lent, go to a fish fry. The fish is not the point. Seeing a community work together to feed the multitudes is a miracle in itself. You don't have to like fish to check it out. It doesn't have to be a fish fry necessarily, it can be any community-feeding project.

**Habitat for Humanity** Spend a day at a Habitat for Humanity project in your community. Take tools, food, or whatever is most needed for the day that you can contribute. There is always a need for whatever assistance you can offer on projects like this.

**Help a Neighbor** Do you have a neighbor for whom you can rake leaves, plant flowers, shovel some snow, or help fix something that is broken? Maybe they are an older person, a single mom, or someone who is sick. Spread the joy!

**Just Serve!** Most churches have multiple places where they need people to help. It could be greeting at the door together or serving in children's ministry with the youth. You could usher, sing in the choir, or any number of things. The most important thing is that you do it together.

**Letter to God** Sit down together, spend some time in reflection, and then each of you write a letter to God. Tell Him what is most important to you or what you most need. Then share your letters with each other, and spend some time praying and sending your letters to God.

**Marriage Group** Join a marriage group in your church and learn some ways to make your marriage great. Then practice the ideas you have learned as you spend time sharing hopes and dreams with each other.

**Mission Statement** Lots of businesses and organizations have taken the time to write out a mission statement. Why not spend some time on a special date where you sit down together and write a mission statement for your marriage? What is your purpose in the life you share together? What are the guiding principles and values that you will follow? How can you be united in your vision and purpose in this partnership? This can be powerful for months and years to come!

**Mission Trip** See if your church sends out short-term mission teams. Pick a country of special interest and sign up to become a part of that team. Usually there are team meetings in advance of the trip. The trip might be educational, to help with construction, or medical in nature, so find one that's a good fit for your talents. It's a great way to make a difference in the world.

**Neighborhood Walk** Choose a poor neighborhood in your community and take a walk through the neighborhood. See if you can feel Christ's presence there, perhaps leading you to do something that will make a small difference. Maybe you'll even have a big idea of how you can get others to help.

**Nursing Home** Visit a nursing home or senior residence, and take some fun with you. Just visiting lonely people goes a long way, but keep the spirit positive. If you have an instrument, take it along and play something. It doesn't have to be professional. It will be the best they have heard in weeks or months.

**Pickup** Find a neighborhood or a street that has become littered, grab a garbage bag, and see how big a difference you can make in even a short while. Give a prize for the strangest item found and for the most garbage collected. It's fun, and you're doing service in your community! Don't expect to receive any praise; just know in your heart that you made a small difference.

**Prayer and Reflection** Set aside a quiet hour from your everyday life where you can both spend some time in prayer and reflection, maybe reading a Bible passage or devotional book.

Then do some journaling, and write down what you are experiencing and what it means to you. Share your journals, and pray with each other. This could become so meaningful you will want to repeat it often.

**Project Child** Plan a project where you can raise some money. Donate it to your favorite charity that feeds hungry children either here or in another part of the world. Maybe even provide regular support for a child through one of these organizations. You'll get to see how he or she grows to become more than they ever could without your support.

**Quiet Reflection** Find an empty, open church. Sit, kneel, explore, and pray. Let peace and reverence seep into your being. Quietly pray for each other. If you like, discuss your deepest spiritual beliefs afterward.

**Salvation Army** Volunteer to serve together at the Salvation Army. Take time to prepare by doing something for someone who has less than you.

**Sharing the Bible** The Bible may not seem like a date book, but try sharing your favorite passage with each other. Don't have a favorite passage? Explore the Song of Songs together.

**Soup Kitchen** Check out a local soup kitchen or homeless shelter, and see what they most need in the way of volunteers. Then plan a date where you can serve together in the area of greatest need. Talk about your experience together afterward and plan a return trip.

**Spiritual Nurture** Do something to nurture your spiritual life. Go to a church service, spend an hour in silence to reflect on some of the great hymns of faith, or chose a special scripture or hymn to share with each other.

**Thanksgiving Board** Sit down together for an evening or a Saturday, and create a "Thanksgiving board" for your marriage and family. Write down notes of what you are thankful for, and pin them to the board. Once the board is filled, hang it in a prominent place where you can refer to it again and again as you continue to remember how you have been blessed. Continue to add new notes from time to time. When discouraged, refer to your board and know that you are blessed.

**Turkey Day** Look for a church or community group that is planning to feed the hungry on Thanksgiving Day. Offer to cook a turkey or some vegetables, and help by taking the food to hungry families. Give thanks with each other for your own blessings as you receive and share joy with others.

**Whatever!** Find a poor family, a sick neighbor, or a single mom, and find out how you can best help. It could be some yard work, minor repairs, or baby-sitting for an evening. There are a number of ways to make a difference. There are people all around you who could use some help. And best of all, you will feel great as you share this time with others.

**Women's Shelter** Find a local women's shelter, and contact them to see what they most need. Sometimes is it simple toiletries, like diapers or toilet paper. Donate some time, and see if you can get some friends and neighbors to help contribute.

# Group Dating Ideas

While we have already listed many dates that could become double dates or even group dates, I am listing a few ideas to add to this possibility. When you have your weekly date, it is important for you to focus on the two of you, but it can be fun occasionally to share your special time with a group or another couple.

**Barbeque** Plan a backyard barbecue for several couples. Each couple could be responsible for a dish. Have some backyard games ready, like croquet, badminton, horseshoes, or corn toss. End the evening with a CD and some favorite songs you can sing.

**Bigger or Better** Directions: each couple starts with something small, and then goes door-to-door in your neighborhood to trade up. Ask people to trade you for something bigger or better than the item. At the end of a specified amount of time, gather together as a group, and vote on who got the biggest and best item.

**Cookie Dough** For a creative group date, go on a scavenger hunt in your neighborhood to find all the ingredients you need to make cookies. When the cookies are made, take them to a mutual friend or maybe a grandparent.

**Dollar Date** Start with a main dish (like pizza) and then go to the store and give each person one dollar. Then let each person choose something (for a dollar or less) to have with your main dish.

**Fondue Party** Have a fondue party. Get a good fondue recipe (they are easily found online), and have a fondue dinner or fondue desserts.

**Green Eggs and Ham** Prepare a ham basted with green dye, and make some green-colored eggs. Each person or couple should bring a favorite Dr. Seuss book along. Of course, *Green Eggs and Ham* will be among the books read. Read the books while dinner is served or as an after-dinner event.

**Have a LAN Party** Plan a computer-game night with everyone playing at the same place. This can be fun even if you don't normally enjoy video games. Just laugh together, and have a good time.

**Hide-and-Seek** Take several couples to Walmart or a large department store. You and your date are the team who hides, and the other couples see which one is the first to find you. Then change who hides and repeat.

**Kidnapping** This can be fun when done by either men or women. A group of guys or girls go out and kidnap their dates, blind-fold them, and tell them it's going to be fun. Then surprise them by taking them to a special picnic at the park or some other event that is planned in advance. It's fun with a group, or it can be a romantic one-on-one date.

**Marshmallow Contest** Have a marshmallow eating contest. See who in the group can fit the most in their mouth!

**Miniature Golf** This works best with just two or three couples. Have the couples keep score by counting both partners, and see who wins. Losers have to treat everyone to ice cream cones or another treat.

**Movie Deception** Go with your date to a movie one night with a big group of friends, but instead of staying and watching the movie, you and your date ditch the group. Plan ahead to find somewhere calm and quite to be alone, and stash a blanket and a picnic basket beforehand so everything is ready for you and your date's arrival. Inside the basket should be a heart-shaped food, and something to drink (simple stuff, be creative). You and your date will have a great time under the stars cuddled up on a blanket, and afterward you'll have a fantastic story to tell to your friends, who were wondering where in the world you two went.

**Picture Scavenger Hunt** Double-date by splitting into couples and venturing off to take pictures within a defined area. Then everyone will reconvene at a predetermined time to share the pictures. Swap cameras with the other couple, go out again, and see who can come back with a duplicate picture of one or more of the sites. The couple with the most duplicate photos is the winner.

**Pizza Party** Have a party with several couples and ask each one to bring their favorite beverage to go with pizza. Order several different pizzas and after you eat ask each couple to share some great experience they have had in their marriage. It could be an adventure, or something that makes their marriage special.

**Play Live Clue** This one requires some creativity. Directions: hand out clues to each individual in the group (location, weapon, and killer, just like the board game). Ask each other questions to try to determine the killer. This can be a lot of fun but requires some creativity and preparation.

**Progressive Dinner** Having a "progressive dinner" is always fun for several couples. Have one course at each person's house as you travel from one to the next. Have the final couple plan some games everyone can play or even a set of questions for each person to answer that will be fun and insightful.

**Survivor Date** Double-date (or include several couples), and select some activities such as games, puzzles, or eating contests. Have a competition with the other couple (or couples) that eliminates the losers to see who "survives" with the highest score. You can make it interesting by putting something at stake, like losing couple buys dessert.

**Theme Party** Throw a theme party like Hawaiian, Italian, French, redneck, Mexican, or cowboy. Plan to dress according to the theme. The food will, of course, represent the theme as well. Each couple can bring one of the courses. Add music to match the theme and plan some appropriate games.

**Video Scavenger Hunt** Directions: each team has a video camera and a list of scenarios to catch on video. Here are a few possible ideas: interview a complete stranger about something random, find a random stranger and greet them like an old friend, stage a break up by yelling at each other and draw lots of attention, or try on clothing for the opposite sex. As you can tell, this can be a ton of fun, especially when you go back and watch your footage.

**Waffle Party** Have a "bring your own topping" waffle party. Assign each group member to bring his or her favorite waffle toppings.

**Water Balloon Volleyball** Have an outdoor water balloon volleyball date. Directions: several couples stand on each side of a volleyball net. Each couple holds a towel stretched between them. Throw and catch the water balloon using only the towels. Have a number of water balloons ready. When one breaks, use the next one. Be prepared to get wet, but that is part of the fun.

**<u>Wii Olympics</u>** Get a group together and have a competition using Wii Sports. You could go through a succession of different sports, develop a scoring system for each couple, or just have some individual competition.

# Getaways and Play Days

While it is important to have a regular date life, it is just as important to have occasional play days and getaways. At least once a quarter, you should plan a getaway just to be together. It can be as simple as spending a whole day together or going away for a night or more. My wife and I have made it a practice to have extended dates at least a few times every year, and we try to have at least one or two weeks away by ourselves every year. I began this book by describing our return home from one of our getaways and the list we created of special times we had shared. In the following section you will find fifty of our dates and getaways that have been memorable times for us, some of which may have been listed in other sections of this book but are also included here.

Don't just duplicate what we have done; instead, use these ideas as a springboard for you to plan your own extended times together. Commit to getting away by yourselves (without your family) several times each year. You can really get in touch with what is special about each other, and build a deeper and more meaningful love affair that can truly last a lifetime.

In fact, I have counseled many couples to have an affair with each other every few years. Turn on your creative imagination and start doing all of the fun and exciting things that couples do when they are having an affair. Try sneaking away to be by yourselves, planning some secret rendezvous, or meeting at a hotel and spending the night. You get the picture. It's amazing how much life you can breathe into your marriage by doing this. I am constantly amazed at how many creative ideas two people who have lived in a boring marriage can come up with as they engage in an affair. If you have an affair with your spouse, you will not likely be tempted to have one with someone else. Marriage at its best should be as exciting and fun as any affair could possibly be, and best of all, it will be guilt-free.

If you say you can't afford all of this, keep in mind how costly it is to go through a divorce. You can divorce proof your marriage by making romance a lifestyle, continually doing new things together, and going all out to make your marriage both fun and fulfilling.

**Air Show** Every now and again you will find an air show in your area or nearby. These are exciting to watch as different formations fly by, one after another. Great fun!

**Alaska** A cruise to or from Alaska can be spectacular. You'll visit coves and view the glaciers break apart and come crashing into the water. You might also take a land trip across part of Alaska on an open-view train with its own dining car. Spend a couple of nights at a lodge, and go off in a search for wildlife, like moose and bears. Go whale watching, or visit a musher camp and let the sled dogs give you a ride on a buggy as you envision yourself on a sled riding through the snow. Enjoy watching the salmon try to jump up small waterfalls, or just enjoy a freshly cooked salmon dinner by the water. There is no end to the fun you can have in Alaska.

**Antigua** Get a taste of a beautiful island with a trip to Antigua, Bermuda, or a different island in the Caribbean. Spend the days exploring or just resting on the beach. Go snorkeling over reefs, and see if you can count the different kinds of colored fish you see. Spend the evenings with dinner and dancing, maybe under the stars on a balmy night. Take lots of pictures so you can recapture the experience in the months and years to come. If you are in Bermuda, you can always travel on a moped built for two.

**Basketball Games** For our wedding anniversary one year, my wife bought us season tickets to our local college basketball games. She didn't even like basketball, but knew I loved it. As one season gave way to the next, she grew to love basketball and has become a loyal and enthusiastic fan. You don't have to limit yourselves to home games; this can extend to away games and tournaments as well. The point here is not the basketball, but starting something together that can become a continual opportunity for dates, even an occasional over-nighter. It could be another sport, something musical, or art or antiques. This can become something special that you do many, many times over the years.

**Bed and Breakfast** Rent a luxury car for the day, pack a bag, and hit the road. Drive until you find a cute bed-and-breakfast, or better yet, make a reservation in advance. (You can check a visitor's center or a welcome center in your state to find a list.) Enjoy the drive, the car, and then have a great time at a romantic B&B. Savor the time you share at a great breakfast in the morning, and linger over your final cup of coffee. Return home the next day with a great memory.

**Blackberry Picking** Grab a bucket or cut open a gallon milk jug with a handle, and head for a mountain path. It won't be hard to find some wild blackberries growing along the road or trail. Be careful the blackberry bushes don't entangle you. Long sleeves are best. Once you fill your jug, head back for some berries and cream, put them on ice cream, or better yet, make a blackberry pie.

**Boat Cruise** Many lakes offer boat cruises for a couple of hours where you can see all the houses on the lake and visit quiet coves and inlets. Many lakes, even large ones, were manmade at some time, flooding large areas of civilization. Some places offer a cocktail hour or dinner on the cruise. Relax and enjoy.

**Canoeing on the Broad River** By now you have figured out that a lot of our dating fun revolves around water. Almost anything on or near water will do. One of our best canoe outings was when we paddled down the Broad River, going by the Biltmore Mansion in Asheville. The river was in a gentle phase, and the quiet water lapping against the canoe just added to the fun. Of course, you might get a wake-up call as you hit a rapid, but once you're through it, you can relax again. Spending a couple of days there can make it all the more special.

**Clues to Romance** Go out in advance and place clues at special places you have both shared, and have your spouse follow from one clue to the next. The last clue should lead them to a hotel where you have booked a room (or the honeymoon suite) and made reservations for a special dinner. Of course, you will both want to have your phones ready for some assistance with clues so you don't end up with an empty hotel room and dinner by yourself.

**Conference or Retreat Center** There are conference and retreat centers that have musical programs that make a great date. Plan to go for a night or two, and enjoy the concert and the time away from everyone else.

**Cottage** Have a friend who owns a getaway cabin? Make arrangements to rent it for a weekend. It might be less expensive than a commercial rental and even more fun. If you can find one on the ocean or some water, all the better. Just enjoy your time together without all the normal distractions. Better yet, leave your cell phones at home or in the car.

**Cruise Ships** Whether or not you live near a cruise port, check out the last minute cruise deals you can find at a nearby port. (Usually the prices drop as the sailing date nears.) You may just want to book a cruise to nowhere and enjoy the ship. Even a three-day cruise can be fun. Or, plan for the cruise of a lifetime—to Europe, Alaska, or some faraway place. Enjoy the shows, the food, and the fun. You will come home with some great memories that you will be talking about for years. Of course, you may need to drop a few pounds when you return.

**Dancing** It can be fun to go dancing almost anywhere, and there are all kinds of dances to enjoy. We will never forget dancing outdoors with the moon reflecting over the water in Antigua. It was our anniversary and Thanksgiving. We had a wonderful dinner and an unforgettable night of dancing under the stars. How much more romantic can it get than that?

**Disney Adventure** While family trips to Disney are great fun, exploring Disney World is just as fun for couples. You may prefer Epcot over the Magic Kingdom, where you can wander through the various countries and explore history, crafts, and dining. Even the Magic Kingdom can be fun if you enjoy roller coasters and other rides. Sea World is another great place to spend time. Swim with the dolphins, play golf, and eat all the time. The Holy Land Experience is another whole day of reflection, powerful shows, and spiritual challenge. Then maybe schedule a low-key day to rest and relax.

**Fall Foliage** Take a drive into the mountains or wherever the leaves are turning their spectacular colors of red, orange, and yellow. Add some evergreens, blue skies, and soft breezes, and you've got a view to remember. Stop often to take some pictures. Enjoy lunch at a mountain chalet. Spend a night or two as you thank God for creating such beautiful seasonal changes and for the opportunity to just be there sharing it together.

**Fireworks** There are always fireworks on the Fourth of July, but there are many places that have fireworks on a regular basis during the year, like ball fields or sporting events. Find a place where you can get a great view, sit back, and relax. Maybe you can eat out before the display or get something afterward.

**Florida Keys** Fly to Miami and rent a car you can use to travel through the Florida Keys. Stop at different scenic places along the way and sample the local cuisine. Pick a hotel and spend a night or two, and then end your journey in Key West. Of course you will drive back the same route, so you can stop and see what you missed on the way down.

**Garden Tours** There are many special gardens around. Some are full plantations, and others specialize in spring flowers, like tulips. Some have a full array of activities you can do while you are there. Some have boating or kayaking, some may have a petting zoo, and others have restaurants.

**Golfing Vacation** Find a location that has several golf courses, and plan a vacation in that area, perhaps at a resort. Play a different golf course each day, with a break in between for rest and other fun. Enjoy the beauty, not just the golf. Don't be preoccupied with the score (or you could decide to spoil the day); just enjoy the fun of being together in such a beautiful place. Of course, the restaurants and shopping are all a part of it. If you don't like golf, it doesn't matter. Just find something else that is fun, like searching out beautiful waterfalls.

**Go to a Zoo** We have visited a number of zoos. It was a different experience to visit a zoo in Colorado where they had the largest collection of giraffes in any zoo, breeding them for other zoos. We went up on a higher level, with lettuce as food, and fed them from our hands as we towered above them. It gave us a whole new perspective on what it means to be too tall. Of course, the other animals were also fun.

**Helicopter Flight** Nothing beats a helicopter flight over the Grand Canyon for pure amazement. What a magnificent place to visit! Seeing the Grand Canyon at the break of day or in an evening sunset is more majestic than you can imagine. There are some great lodges where you can stay with some wonderful dining. If you want to stay there, you must book well in advance, but it's worth it.

**House Tours** Check your community for house tours. They may be new homes in an upscale development, historic houses in your community, or decorated houses for a season like Christmas. Sometimes you may be able to go inside as well. You may even get an idea you would like to add to your own home.

**Intracoastal Waterway** You can have a great trip cruising the Intracoastal Waterway. Check out the "dock and dine" restaurants along the way, or cook some of your own food on board. Have fun taking turns at the wheel and the charts, and stop to watch the dolphins play. Tie up for the night, plug in your air conditioning, and sleep through the night with the sound of small waves lapping against the boat. Depending on the time of year, watch for approaching storms, and make sure your anchor holds well. You can do this for a couple of days or make it into a longer journey, like from New York to South Carolina (as we have done) or all the way to Florida.

You don't have to travel all that distance; any time on the waterway can be fun in a boat.

**Island Resort** Check out vacation time in Jamaica or one of the islands. Book your flights, and enjoy a week at an exotic resort. You will be able to visit some wonderful spots: beautiful waterfalls, great dining, and perhaps a great view of the stars. Make it the romantic special for the year.

**Lake Powell** As a part of a Western trip, don't miss boating on Lake Powell. It is a magical trip through many beautiful canyons that are carved out of colored rocks. Each view seems more impressive than the previous one. You will be amazed at how a larger boat can squeeze through a narrow passageway. This makes a great day trip, and you can spend the night in a nearby lodge or hotel.

**Love Nature?** Rent a car and travel through beautiful Sequoia National Park, and then on to King's Canyon. Walk (or even drive) through those magnificent trees that have been there forever. Hike through the forest to get a closer view of a waterfall. See if a chipmunk will come to your picnic to sample some of your lunch. Take picture after picture so you can get another glimpse of the magnificent beauty when you return home.

**Lunch Date Special** We were swimming one morning when we talked about where we might go for lunch. We decided on lunch at a marina so we could enjoy the water. This led to checking out some condos that were on the water, and we left, inspired to move there. We became more realistic later, and decided to stay where we were, but this was a really fun date that almost changed our lives. No end to possibilities here.

**Major-League Baseball** Take a trip to a major-league baseball town. Get your tickets, find a nice place to stay, and head for the ball field. Enjoy everything about it—the hot dogs, ice cream, crowds, noise, and the cheering. Stay for a night or two in the town for a break from day-to-day life before returning home.

**Mansions** Go someplace where you can visit a mansion, like the Biltmore Mansion, or a place like Newport, where there is a whole row of mansions. There are places all over the world. Spend some time seeing how the really wealthy have lived, and then be thankful that you don't have to clean all those bedrooms and baths.

**Mission Trip** One of our most memorable getaways was when we decided to join a mission team to Haiti. We spent a week at an orphanage singing and playing with children. We were there to share the love of God with a forgotten people. It was just after a big earthquake, and our eyes were opened to the vast destruction that occurred, as blockhouse after blockhouse (by the thousands) had fallen down and given way to villages of tents. So many lives had been lost in a place where it was difficult to live even before the disaster. We will never forget the smiles and laughter of those children; they enriched our lives perhaps even more than we enriched theirs. This is a great way to enrich your marriage. Spend a week some place where the need is great, and find a way to make even a small difference.

**Moonlight Sailing** Many places have good-sized sailboats and offer sunset or moonlight cruises. Nothing beats the quiet of a sailboat as you only hear the waves lapping against the boat. Moonlight and evening breezes make it all the more special. What could be more romantic than that?

**Music Festivals** There are cities that have special music festivals in the United States and all over the world. Plan your trip to coincide with an event, and see what other activities might be a part of the trip. You will find music, theater, food, and dancing from all over. Make it the trip of a lifetime or the best trip of the year.

**New York City** New York is always fun to visit, but it becomes especially magical during the Christmas season. The department store windows are all aglow, the tree in Rockefeller Center is beautifully lighted, and the ice skaters are doing their twirls. Take a carriage ride through Central Park. Get tickets to see the Rockettes do their kicking, or take in a Broadway show. There is no end to the restaurants. You can dine at the top of a skyscraper, or see all the lights from the Empire State Building. Few things can be more romantic than a trip to NYC at Christmas.

**Outdoor Musical** Check your area for outdoor musical theater. Get tickets ahead of time, get in the car, and go. The fun is in the time away, but it is even more fun as you enjoy the musical, play, or outdoor festival. There is always a new show somewhere.

**Pike's Peak** Want to climb to the top of a mountain but aren't up to it? Then take a drive to the top of Pike's Peak, Colorado, and look over the vast landscape below you. Of course, there may be some clouds below you that are blocking the view. Take your picture, raising your hand, as you stand at the top. (You don't have to tell anyone you got there by car.) Be careful of those who are racing down the mountain on bicycles. You can always take in the Garden of the Gods at you come down the mountain. This is a series of beautiful peaks that rise straight up out of the ground in a collection of "gods" that seem to guard the territory.

**Quiet Cove** Take your boat (or rent one if you need to), and find a quiet cove in a beautiful location. Drop the anchor, and kick back and enjoy a lunch on the water. Maybe you will take a little nap before you return, or go overboard for a short swim. Watch for the wildlife; you're bound to view things you don't normally see. Don't be in a hurry to get back to port.

**San Francisco** Visit a city like San Francisco and spend a few days exploring. Enjoy the trolley rides, watch the sea lions, have some great food, and walk the streets. Some might even want to add a little shopping along the way.

**Statue of Liberty** Take a boat into New York Harbor to watch fireworks around the Statue of Liberty on the Fourth of July or another special celebration. It can be the most spectacular fireworks display ever. Or, if you can't make New York, take a boat just off shore where there are fireworks in many places on the Fourth of July. Seeing the fireworks over the water adds a whole new dimension to the enjoyment.

**Summer Theater** Many communities have "summer stock" or outdoor theater productions that make a great date. Find one near you, and enjoy not only the event but the special time for the two of you to just be with each other.

**Swiss Alps** While planning special vacations together, don't forget the beauty and majesty of the Swiss Alps. Rent an auto, and drive from one beautiful place to the next. You might even take in a cultural celebration and parade. The food is a whole other story, but the picturesque villages are a great place to spend some extra time. You might even take a daytrip into Germany and visit a castle, or head into Austria for some great music. You will want to bring home some special wood-carvings and other things of interest that you will treasure.

**Tea Garden/Winery** Visit a tea plantation and sample some special teas. If there is no tea garden near you, see if you can find a local winery that offers tours and samples of wines. Top it all off with a lunch at some quaint or picturesque restaurant.

**Time-Shares** Many resorts offer time-shares and would love to have you become a time-share owner at some significant cost. However, there are a lot of beautiful resorts where you can pick up a resale week for free or very little money. You will have to pay yearly maintenance fees, but you will have the opportunity to spend a week there every year, or trade into another resort in some other location. This can be a great time if you want a week in a beautiful resort for a substantially less investment. Just being away with each other for a week is a great opportunity for some deeper sharing and renewed commitment.

**Trail Ride** There are many mountain areas where you can book a full trail ride in some of the most beautiful country in the world. Riding the horses is only part of the fun. Seeing some spectacular scenery only adds to the experience. Maybe you will have a trail guide who will display his skill at some campfire cooking before you return.

**Trip to the Holy Land** Check with your church (or other churches in the area) to see when the next trip to the Holy Land will be. Plan on a full week to visit the many places where Jesus ministered to the people, fed the thousands, preached the Beatitudes, and spent time on the Sea of Galilee. You won't want to miss the boat trip across the Sea of Galilee, maybe even be baptized in the Jordan River. Jerusalem is a wonderful place to explore; there are so many meaningful sites. Don't miss the Gethsemane Garden among the ancient olive trees and, of course, the Garden Tomb. It would be a trip of a lifetime, with so many, many memories. You might even add an addition to the trip so you could cruise the Greek Islands for a couple of days.

**Tubing in Helen** If you want a great place to go tubing down the river, you might plan a trip to Helen, Georgia. The whole town is built like an alpine village and features beautifully decorated cottages and shops. There are thousands of large tubes and rafts to rent so you can tube down the mostly lazy river. However, there are some places where you have to hold your breath and hang on as you go down a large rapid and nearly tip over. It's all part of the fun. You may want to do it again the next day. Try some new German dishes or some fantastic desserts. Pick up a few things from the many alpine shops.

**Warships** Many communities with ocean access have warship touring available. It could be an aircraft carrier, destroyer, or even a submarine. Usually there are tour guides available who can share the history of that ship and the battles it was in. There may be a movie that will add to the historical information. Do a little research ahead of time to fully appreciate the part that ship played in the wars for our freedom.

**Waterfront Restaurants** We have always enjoyed dining on the water. It is a lot of fun to get in our boat and head off to a waterfront restaurant with docking and dining. There is something special about getting off a boat as you enter a restaurant. It is a different feeling. Then you can continue to enjoy the water as you return home. You might head home the same day, or you might extend the trip a night or two and repeat the experience.

**White Water Rafting** Find a river that has some white water rafting. Go with some others (and a guide if need be), and have fun crashing through the rapids and down some small waterfalls. Paddle like crazy to keep on the right part of the river so you don't get hung up or tipped over. Don't close your eyes just because you see a big one coming. It's full-time alert, but so much fun. Check out the difficulty of that stretch of white water before deciding you are ready for it, and then give it all you've got.

**Wildlife Exposition** People gather from all over the country for a wildlife exposition. There will be paintings of wildlife, winning photographs, carvings, and special activities for all. You will be amazed at the creativity of talented people. Spend a couple of days just taking it all in. You may even buy something special for your home.

**Yacht Dining** Find someone who has a big yacht, and see if you can arrange to have a catered dinner at sunset or inside by candlelight. Pretend that you are on a world cruise, and talk about all the special places you would like to visit.

# Conclusions

**The Ultimate** One time, my wife and I were at a marriage retreat, and the male leader got all of us guys together and challenged us to provide a tidal wave of love for our wives. The assignment was to buy a gift and a love card for our wives each day for forty days. After seeing this start to happen, my wife's expectation was that it would end after a week or maybe ten days. When it went on and on for forty days, it became a memory that has never faded. The hard part was finding forty love cards, and I had to go to several card shops to find that many. The gifts ranged from something like a bathrobe, a kitchen utensil, or some makeup, to tickets to a movie, jewelry, and ended in a final love letter. There are many variations on this theme, but it will be a memory that is never forgotten.

The "tidal wave" was neither a date nor a getaway; it was a forty-day period of expressing love in some tangible ways. In that period there were a number of dates. It began the week before Valentine's Day. Migsie thought surely it would end on that day when we did have a special date; however, it went on and on. She hated to see it end, as she said, "You better warn me when this is coming to an end, because I've been getting used to this!"

This was the hardest thing I had done, of all the dates and trips you have read about in these pages. You must go to card shops to find forty cards that express sincere love but not special occasion cards like birthdays or mother's day. Then get and wrap forty gifts, one to go with each card, without breaking the bank. The secret to this whole experience was that it forced me to be creative. Each day was new. There were no repeat performances. I had to find many ways to express my love for Migsie.

Why do I tell you this? It's because marriage is a long journey of expressing love to the same person, day after day, in a thousand different ways. Not just ways that are meaningful to me, but in ways that are meaningful to her; ways that speak her love language. I've spent thousands of hours counseling couples who have failed to learn this. Their marriages have gradually eroded from the excitement of their first date and the special day of the wedding, to the dreariness of day-to-day living. The bottom line for so many is this: Do you still love your spouse? Do you love your spouse as much as you used to? I never want Migsie to look into my eyes with tears and question my love, as I have seen so many couples do.

I truly believe that God wants us to have happy marriages. Dating is not the answer to all marriage issues, of course. But when couples are constantly spending time together having fun, doing new things, and enjoying each other, it is much easier to resolve issues in the spirit of love rather than in a time of bitter conflict.

I'm not sure I should have included a section on "romantic dates." As you have read through this resource manual I'm sure you have seen romantic dates in every section. Any time you can look into each other's eyes, whether standing by a beautiful waterfall or after a sweaty workout, and can say, "I really love you! I love being with you! I love doing things with you! I would be lost without you," it will be romantic. It's a matter of a deep, heartfelt connection, belonging to each other, and being comfortable with each other. You don't build this in one or two dates but over years of dating; years of making each other feel more special each day as your love grows and grows. I always conclude my marriage seminars or teaching courses by telling couples to make romance a lifestyle. It is not a special moment, though there are many of those, but a lifetime of pouring your love into that special person you have married. Then in many respects, marriage will be one long, lifetime date—always new, always fresh, always fun, and always overflowing with love.

That has been our experience and we want it to be yours. It's up to you to accept the challenge!

Vern and Migsie

**Marriage issues:** If you are having some marriage issues, or would just like to rejuvenate or improve your marriage, you might want to check out my book, *Pathway to a Happy Marriage*. This is designed as a six-week program of marriage counsel and activity to help marriages come alive. It is written as if you were to go to a counselor for six to seven weeks and leads you on a path to a happy marriage. There are assignments and activities included with each weekly session, all pointing toward some serious changes that will enrich your marriage, no matter where you are starting.

If you would like to contact me with any response to this book, or how you have experienced and used these ideas, you may do so by email at vj@datingfunforcouples.com.

Made in the USA
Middletown, DE
22 February 2015